For those seeking to live faithfully with Christ at the center of everyday life.

Copyright

Are You Walking With Jesus: A 60-Day Discipleship Devotional for Prayer, Reflection, and Obedience, by Stephen H Berkey, published by Get Wisdom Publishing, Box 465, Thompsons Station, TN 37179, copyright © 2026, Stephen H Berkey.
Printed in the United States of America

ISBN 978-1-952359-79-8 (paperback)
ISBN 978-1-952359-80-4 (ebook)
Audiobook available (Amazon.com and audible.com)

For more information
about Get Wisdom Publishing:
https://getwisdompublishing.com/

The Wisdom Prayer Series

Are You Walking With Jesus

A 60-Day Discipleship Devotional for Prayer, Reflection, and Obedience

Stephen H Berkey

Free PDF

Life Improvement Principles

[Get the ebook version for 99 cents]

You can live your best life!

Welcome to a journey of discovery! In case you have forgotten, your actions have consequences. Unlock your potential! This book (60+ pages) provides the overview of all our strategies and wisdom principles to live your best life. You *can* transform your life! Get your wisdom-based roadmap to a better life and unlock the possibilities for growth and success.

FREE PDF

https://getwisdompublishing.com/resource-registration/

Kindle ebook for 99 cents:

https://www.amazon.com/dp/B0FG883KZM

Ebook

Free PDF

Make it your life goal to be the best you can be!

Discover Wisdom and live the life you deserve.

Table of Contents

"It Will Change Your Life"

This 60-Day Devotional book will change your life and draw you closer to God!

If you want that to happen just spend 10-15 minutes of serious time with these prayers, reflections, and questions each day for the next 60 days. That's all.

God's wisdom will penetrate you soul!

Special Note:

This book is a Christ-centered, prayer-driven discipleship devotional designed to shape daily obedience, spiritual formation, and long-term faithfulness.

This is not **an inspirational daily lift, a topical Bible study, or a therapeutic self-help devotional.**

My Discipleship Life Prayer

Father, make Jesus the central reality of my life:

1) Ignite in me a deep affection for Jesus, Your Word, and Your will in my life.
2) Fill my heart and mind with Your presence, power, wisdom, and love, in order that I might abide in You, so I can love You with all my heart, mind, body, and soul, and love my neighbor as I love myself.
3) Thank you for Your grace, sacrifice, forgiveness, and the gift of salvation that allows me to live confidently in the family of God.
4) Give me knowledge, understanding, and wisdom to make godly decisions, living in humble obedience to Your ways.
5) Give me strength, patience, and perseverance to reject the foolish values of this world, in order to love and worship You all the days of my life.
6) Produce spiritual fruit in me: love, joy, peace, patience, kindness, goodness, faithfulness, gentleness, and self-control so that I can live and walk by the Spirit, rejecting the sins of my flesh.
7) Allow my words and actions to help others believe the Gospel, drawing them to Christ.
8) Empower me to be bold, stand firm, walk faithfully, and endure all adversity to bring glory to Your Name.
9) Help me to be grateful and satisfied with whatever I have.
10) Lord, I surrender myself fully to You. Please create in me a clean heart, and renew a right and steadfast spirit within me.

Lord, heap blessing on me and my family today; bring peace, contentment, and rest into our lives and homes in order that our faithful service brings glory and honor to Your Name. Amen.

How to Use This Devotional

Are You Walking With Jesus is designed to support a steady and thoughtful rhythm of discipleship rather than a hurried reading plan. The goal is to allow prayer, Scripture, and reflection to shape your devotional life for 60 days.

Each day follows a simple structure:

- **Scripture.**
  Read the selected passage slowly, maybe more than once. Allow the idea to settle in your thoughts.
- **Devotional reflection.**
  The reflection is meant to provide focus and perspective, not exhaustive explanation. Does the theme connect with your current season of life?
- **Questions.**
  Consider the reflection questions. They are meant to encourage honest engagement and practical application.
- **Journaling space.**
  The facing page is provided for personal notes, prayers, or reflections. Make this space work for you.
- **Prayer.**
  The daily prayer can be read as written or adapted into your own words. Let it become a natural response to what you have read and reflected on.

The book is arranged as a 60-day journey through twelve core themes of Christian discipleship. While it is intended for daily use, there is no need to rush or to "catch up" if a day is missed. It can be used at your own pace and revisited at any time.

The book is suitable for individual reflection, mentoring relationships, or small-group use. However you use it, approach each day with openness rather than expectation, trusting God to work patiently and faithfully in your life.

Discipleship is not measured by completion, but by alignment. Allow this devotional to serve as a guide for living with Christ at the center of your everyday life.

The Discipleship Life Prayer
An Invitation

An Invitation to a Christ-Centered Life.

This devotional invites you to consider a simple but life-shaping question: *Are you walking with Jesus?* Over the next sixty days, these prayers and reflections are designed to help you deepen your relationship with Christ, align your heart with His will, and live each day in faithful discipleship.

Discipleship is not primarily about acquiring information or following religious routines. It's about being formed day by day into the likeness of Christ. The Discipleship Life Prayer is offered as a simple and intentional way to align yourself with that purpose.

This prayer is not meant to be recited mechanically or mastered quickly. It is meant to be leaned into. Each line reflects a desire for Christ to become central in your life and for daily life to be shaped by God's wisdom and grace. It recognizes that transformation is not achieved through effort alone, but through ongoing surrender and attentive engagement.

Over the next sixty days, slow down and engage one portion of the prayer at a time. Each day's reading is designed to help you reflect on the meaning of the prayer, consider its implications, and respond thoughtfully. The goal is to live more consistently with what you believe.

The Prayer acknowledges both God's work and our response. It asks God to shape the inner life while calling for faithful action and endurance. It speaks to ordinary moments as well as difficult seasons, offering a steady framework for refection and growth.

The Prayer reflects a way of life that blesses families and homes while bringing glory to God through faithful service. Whether used individually or in community, it offers a rhythm of reflection that can be revisited daily.

May it bless your day,

Steve Berkey

SECTION 1

Jesus at the Center

Prayer Focus:

"Father, make Jesus the central reality of my life"

Day 1
Jesus at the Center

Discipleship Life Prayer Focus
"Father, make Jesus the central reality of my life."

Colossians 1:15–18 The Son is the image of the invisible God, the firstborn over all creation. For in him all things were created: things in heaven and on earth, visible and invisible, whether thrones or powers or rulers or authorities; all things have been created through him and for him. He is before all things, and in him all things hold together. And he is the head of the body, the church . . . so that in everything he might have the supremacy. NIV

Devotional Reflection

Every life has a center, something that inherently organizes priorities, decisions, and hopes. This discipleship prayer begins by asking God to place Jesus in that defining center position. Not as an accessory to life, but as its core. Scripture tells us that Christ is not only Savior, but the One in whom "all things hold together." When Jesus is central, your life begins to make sense.

Making Jesus central is more than belief; it is orientation. It means allowing His truth to shape how we interpret success and failure and how we respond to the world. This prayer acknowledges that without intentional centering on Him our lives will drift toward self-reliance.

Life Implications

A life centered on Jesus develops a natural structure. When Christ is allowed to occupy the defining centerpiece, priorities begin to align and decisions gain clarity. Life becomes less reactive and more anchored, shaped by Jesus. Identity is no longer built on performance or circumstance, but understood through relationship.

The purpose of this prayer is to create a life that increasingly finds stability and meaning in Christ's sustaining presence.

Reflection

1. What most often functions as the center of my life in practice?

2. What would change if Jesus truly defined how I see everything else?

Daily Prayer

Father, make Jesus the central reality of my life today, shaping my priorities, decisions, and perspective.

Notes

Day 2
Recognizing Competing Centers

Discipleship Life Prayer Focus

"Father, make Jesus the central reality of my life."

Matthew 6:21 For where your treasure is, there your heart will be also. NIV
Luke 9:23 Then he said to them all: "Whoever wants to be my disciple must deny themselves and take up their cross daily and follow me." NIV

Devotional Reflection

Jesus warned us that wherever our treasure is, our heart will follow. This devotional invites honest reflection about what competes for the central focus of our lives. Even good things like family, work, responsibility, and ministry can quietly displace Christ if they become too important.

This discipleship prayer does not assume neutrality. It recognizes that the heart is always oriented toward something. Jesus' call to deny self and follow Him is not about self-rejection, it's about refusing to let lesser centers of influence rule our lives. When Christ is displaced, decisions suffer and purpose becomes blurred.

Naming competing centers of influence is not an act of failure; it is an act of clarity. Christ does not shame us for divided hearts, rather He invites us to realign them. This prayer asks God to expose what has taken undue weight and to gently restore Jesus to His rightful place at the center of our life.

Life Implications

You must be aware of what competes for ultimate authority in your life. Over time, awareness will replace denial, and the heart will become more honest about what has authority. When competing influences are named their power diminishes and space is created for realignment. Life grows less anxious and confused as Christ reigns in your life. The implication of this prayer is not the elimination of all other loves, but the proper ordering of them under Jesus' leadership.

Reflection

1. What currently commands most of my attention, energy, or concern?

2. Where might I need to loosen my grip so Christ can lead more fully?

Daily Prayer

Father, reveal what competes for my heart and restore Jesus to His rightful place at the center of my life.

Notes

Day 3
Living Under Christ's Lordship

Discipleship Life Prayer Focus
"Father, make Jesus the central reality of my life."

Romans 14:8–9 If we live, we live for the Lord; and if we die, we die for the Lord. So, whether we live or die, we belong to the Lord. For this very reason, Christ died and returned to life so that he might be the Lord of both the dead and the living. NIV

Devotional Reflection

Making Jesus central is to live consistently under His lordship. This means acknowledging that life ultimately belongs to Him, not just during spiritual moments, but in everyday choices and responsibilities. Scripture reminds us that whether we live or die, we belong to the Lord.

Lordship is not about control for its own sake, it's about trust. When Jesus is Lord we no longer carry the full weight for the direction of our lives. Decisions are shaped by His wisdom. Our identity is rooted in His calling rather than performance. Obedience becomes an expression of our relationship, not the result of obligation.

This prayer invites us to stop negotiating authority with Christ but to conform to His leadership. A life under His lordship may not be easier, but it is free from the burden of being its own master.

Life Implications

Living under Christ's lordship gradually reshapes how authority, responsibility, and freedom are understood. Over time, life becomes less driven by self-protection and more guided by trust. Decisions are approached with humility rather than urgency. Identity is increasingly grounded in following rather than achievement. As Christ's lordship is embraced daily, life becomes steadier and more focused.

Reflection

1. In what areas do I resist Christ's authority most?
2. What would trusting His lordship look like for me today?

Daily Prayer

Lord Jesus, I surrender my authority to You and trust Your leadership in every part of my life today.

Notes

Day 4
Re-Centering a Drifting Heart

Discipleship Life Prayer Focus
"Father, make Jesus the central reality of my life."

Hebrews 12:1–2 Therefore, since we are surrounded by such a great cloud of witnesses, let us throw off everything that hinders and the sin that so easily entangles. And let us run with perseverance the race marked out for us, fixing our eyes on Jesus, the pioneer and perfecter of faith. . . . NIV

Devotional Reflection

Even sincere disciples drift and accumulate distraction. Life pressures multiply slowly, almost unnoticed. Christ can drift from the center to the background. Drift is part of the human condition and re-centering is part of faithful discipleship.

Scripture urges us to fix our eyes on Jesus, not because we have failed, but because focus on Him restores clarity. Re-centering is not about guilt, but about realignment. It occurs through humble intentionality, returning to prayer, reading Scripture, and conforming to His ways.

This Discipleship Life Prayer becomes a daily recalibration: "Father, bring me back to what matters most." Christ does not require perfection, but welcomes our return when we have been distracted. Each re-centering moment is an act of trust, a statement that Jesus remains worthy of first place in our lives.

Life Implications

When you have re-centered your life you will learn to recognize drift without fear or shame. Attentiveness to Him will overcome complacency and returning to Christ becomes a practiced rhythm rather than a crisis response. Focus is restored through repeated attention to what matters most. The implication of this prayer is a life that remains spiritually responsive. That means we are quick to return, willing to refocus, and confident that Christ is worthy of the center of our lives, no matter the circumstances.

Reflection

1. Where do I sense spiritual drift in my life right now?
2. What practice helps me refocus on Christ most effectively?

Daily Prayer

Father, when my heart drifts, gently draw me back and refocus my life on Jesus.

Notes

Day 5
When Christ Defines Reality

Discipleship Life Prayer Focus
"Father, make Jesus the central reality of my life."

Galatians 2:20 I have been crucified with Christ and I no longer live, but Christ lives in me. The life I now live in the body, I live by faith in the Son of God, who loved me and gave himself for me. NIV

Devotional Reflection

The apostle Paul described a life so centered on Christ that personal identity was transformed: "I no longer live, but Christ lives in me." This is the goal of our discipleship prayer: the creation of a Christ-shaped life.

When Jesus defines reality, circumstances lose their power to determine value or direction. Success does not inflate us and failure does not undo us. Life is defined "by faith in the Son of God," trusting His love and example day by day.

This prayer invites a profound shift. Instead of reacting to life we should respond with Christ-centered confidence. When Jesus is central, life becomes less about control and more about faithfulness. We live with a focus on Him rather than being defined by our circumstances.

Life Implications

When Christ defines reality His perspective gradually becomes our centering core. Circumstances lose their power to determine our worth and hope. Life becomes less governed by success or failure and more determined by trust in Christ's presence and purpose. Identity settles into something steadier than emotion or performance. This prayer is not an escape from difficulty, but a resilient confidence that allows life to be lived faithfully and calmly from a Christ-centered perspective.

Reflection

1. What would change if Christ, not circumstances, defined my reality?

2. How can I consciously live today from faith rather than self-effort?

Daily Prayer

Lord Jesus, help me live today by faith, allowing Your life to shape mine.

Notes

Section 1 — Reflection Summary

Jesus as the Central Reality of Life

Over the past five days, this first section has invited a careful reorientation of life around a single, defining center: Jesus. Rather than addressing behavior first, it has focused on alignment. What organizes priorities, shapes decisions, and gives coherence to daily life? To make Jesus the central reality is not to add something new, but to recognize what must rightly hold first place.

Centering life on Christ is less about intensity and more about clarity. When Jesus is central in your life, identity stabilizes and our direction becomes clearer. Competing pressures lose some of their power. This section has acknowledged that drift is normal, that competing influences are subtle, and that re-centering is not a one-time act but an ongoing practice.

Living under Christ's lordship does not remove our responsibility, but rather reshapes it. Authority is entrusted to Christ rather than on circumstances. Faith becomes less reactive and more grounded. As time passes this focus on Christ brings a steady confidence.

We have affirmed that re-centering is always possible. A drifting heart is not a failed heart. Rather, the invitation is to fix our eyes again on Christ so we are rooted in His grace.

As you pause here, consider not what you have *done* during these days, but what may have changed.

Reflection

- Where have I noticed subtle drift? What will help me return my focus to Christ?
- How might my decisions look different if Christ was clearly emphasized more each day?

My Closing Response

Father, continue to shape my life around what matters. Bring clarity where there has been drift, and steadiness where there has been strain. Teach me to live with Jesus at the center, trusting that all else finds its rightful place in Him.

Notes

My Discipleship Life Prayer

Father, make Jesus the central reality of my life:

1) Ignite in me a deep affection for Jesus, Your Word, and Your will in my life.
2) Fill my heart and mind with Your presence, power, wisdom, and love, in order that I might abide in You, so I can love You with all my heart, mind, body, and soul, and love my neighbor as I love myself.
3) Thank you for Your grace, sacrifice, forgiveness, and the gift of salvation that allows me to live confidently in the family of God.
4) Give me knowledge, understanding, and wisdom to make godly decisions, living in humble obedience to Your ways.
5) Give me strength, patience, and perseverance to reject the foolish values of this world, in order to love and worship You all the days of my life.
6) Produce spiritual fruit in me: love, joy, peace, patience, kindness, goodness, faithfulness, gentleness, and self-control so that I can live and walk by the Spirit, rejecting the sins of my flesh.
7) Allow my words and actions to help others believe the Gospel, drawing them to Christ.
8) Empower me to be bold, stand firm, walk faithfully, and endure all adversity to bring glory to Your Name.
9) Help me to be grateful and satisfied with whatever I have.
10) Lord, I surrender myself fully to You. Please create in me a clean heart, and renew a right and steadfast spirit within me.

Lord, heap blessing on me and my family today; bring peace, contentment, and rest into our lives and homes in order that our faithful service brings glory and honor to Your Name. Amen.

SECTION 2

Affection for Jesus, His Word, and His Will

Prayer Focus:

"Ignite in me a deep affection for Jesus, Your Word, and Your will in my life."

Day 6
From Duty to Desire

Discipleship Life Prayer Focus
"Ignite in me a deep affection for Jesus."

Psalm 42:1–2 As the deer pants for streams of water, so my soul pants for you, my God. My soul thirsts for God, for the living God. When can I go and meet with God? NIV

Devotional Reflection

Faith can easily drift into routine. Spiritual practices and habits continue, but affection may cool. This discipleship prayer does not demand more effort, but asks Him to awaken our desire. The psalmist compares longing for God to physical thirst—an ache that cannot be ignored. That kind of desire cannot be manufactured. Instead it must be ignited.

God does not shame a dry heart. Instead, He invites honesty. When affection fades, the answer is not forced discipline, but renewed focus and action. Desire grows where attention is given. Time with Christ and openness to His presence will rekindle love that has grown less intense or quiet.

This prayer reminds us that Jesus is not only to be followed, but He is to be worshiped and loved. Love, once awakened, naturally overflows into obedience.

Life Implications

A life shaped by growing affection for Jesus learns to move beyond obligation and toward relationship. Spiritual practices are less about maintaining discipline and more about making room for an encounter with the Divine. Attention given to Christ gradually rekindles spiritual desire, a softened heart, and renewed joy. Motivation shifts from an effort to love because obedience becomes a response rather than a requirement.

The implication of this prayer is the desire for a faith that is increasingly sustained by affection, not endurance.

Reflection Questions

1. Has my faith felt more like duty than desire lately?

2. What draws my heart closer to Jesus when I make space for Him?

Daily Prayer

Father, ignite in me a deeper affection for Jesus, awakening love where my heart has grown quiet.

Notes

Day 7
Loving Jesus Above All Else

Discipleship Life Prayer Focus
"Ignite in me a deep affection for Jesus."

John 21:15–17 When they had finished eating, Jesus said to Simon Peter, 'Simon son of John, do you love me more than these?" Yes, Lord,' he said, 'you know that I love you.' Jesus said, 'Feed my lambs.' Again Jesus said, 'Simon son of John, do you love me?' He answered, 'Yes, Lord, you know that I love you.' Jesus said, 'Take care of my sheep. 'The third time he said to him, 'Simon son of John, do you love me?' Peter was hurt because Jesus asked him the third time, 'Do you love me?' He said, 'Lord, you know all things; you know that I love you.' Jesus said, 'Feed my sheep. NIV

Devotional Reflection

When Jesus restored Peter He did not ask about performance or failure, He asked about love. "Do you love Me?" This still remains the central discipleship question. Affection for Jesus is not optional, it is foundational. Everything else flows from that relationship.

Loving Jesus above all else does not diminish other loves, but rather orders them. When Christ is first, relationships deepen, service becomes joyful, and obedience gains meaning. When He is not, even good things can become burdens.

This prayer invites a simple but searching honesty. The question is not "Do I know the right things?" but "Do I love Him?" Jesus welcomes imperfect love but He does not ignore misplaced priorities. He gently calls the heart back to what matters most.

Life Implications

When love for Jesus is placed above all else, life begins to reorder itself naturally. Competing loves lose their ability to dominate attention or allegiance. Relationships and responsibilities are not diminished. They are encouraged and supported. Devotion becomes more focused, anchored in affection rather than service. The implication of this prayer is a life increasingly guided by love for Christ as the primary reference point for all other commitments.

Reflection Questions

1. What evidence in my life shows that I love Jesus?
2. What other loves might be crowding out deeper affection for Him?

Daily Prayer

Lord Jesus, help me love You above all else, ordering my heart and desires around You.

Notes

Day 8
Delighting in God's Word

Discipleship Life Prayer Focus

"Ignite in me a deep affection for Your Word."

Psalm 1:1–3 Blessed is the one who does not walk in step with the wicked or stand in the way that sinners take or sit in the company of mockers, but whose delight is in the law of the LORD, and who meditates on his law day and night. That person is like a tree planted by streams of water, which yields its fruit in season and whose leaf does not wither – whatever they do prospers. NIV

Devotional Reflection

God's Word was never meant to be merely read; it was meant to be loved and absorbed. Scripture describes a person who delights in God's Word as rooted, nourished, and steady. Delight in Him should change how we approach the Bible because it is life-giving sustenance.

Affection for Scripture grows when it is received as God's voice rather than as just religious material. The Word reveals Christ, shapes wisdom, and anchors the heart. When we delight in it, we are slowly reshaped by it.

This discipleship prayer asks God to move Scripture from the margins into the center of our daily life. He doesn't want us to read mechanically but to listen more expectantly.

Life Implications

A life that delights in God's Word becomes steadily grounded and resilient. The Scriptures move from occasional reference to trusted counsel, shaping perspective and guiding decisions. Delight will foster attentiveness, allowing God's voice to be heard more clearly amid competing messages. As affection for Scripture grows, stability replaces restlessness. The implication of this prayer is that we are nourished by God's Word and sustained through regular engagement.

Reflection Questions

1. How do I typically approach God's Word—with eagerness or obligation?

2. What helps Scripture feel more personal to me?

Daily Prayer

Father, grow my affection for Your Word, that I may delight in it and be shaped by it daily.

Notes

Day 9
Learning to Love God's Will

Discipleship Life Prayer Focus

"Ignite in me a deep affection for Your will in my life."

Psalm 40:8 I desire to do your will, my God; your law is within my heart. NIV
Romans 12:2 Do not conform to the pattern of this world, but be transformed by the renewing of your mind. Then you will be able to test and approve what God's will is – his good, pleasing and perfect will. NIV

Devotional Reflection

God's will is often misunderstood as restrictive, when in truth it is redemptive. This prayer asks not just for obedience to God's will, but affection for it. That is a deeper request because it acknowledges that resistance often lives not in behavior, but in desire.

As our minds are renewed, God reshapes what we want. His will becomes less about loss and more about trust. Loving God's will means believing that He knows what leads to joy, even when His ways challenge our comfort or expectations.

Life Implications

Loving God's will reshapes trust at a foundational level. Resistance gives way to confidence as God's purposes are seen as life-sustaining rather than limiting. Desire slowly aligns with wisdom and obedience becomes an expression of faith rather than reluctance. The heart learns to rest in God's direction, even when our understanding is incomplete. The focus of this prayer is a life increasingly marked by trust and one that welcomes God's will as a reliable guide, rather than a reluctant concession.

Reflection Questions

1. Where do I struggle most to accept God's will?

2. What would change if I trusted His purposes fully?

Daily Prayer

Father, shape my desires so that I may not only obey Your will, but delight in it.

Notes

Day 10
Guarding Against a Cold Heart

Discipleship Life Prayer Focus
"Ignite in me a deep affection for Jesus, Your Word, and Your will."

Revelation 2:4–5 Yet I hold this against you: you have forsaken the love you had at first. Consider how far you have fallen! Repent and do the things you did at first. If you do not repent, I will come to you and remove your lampstand from its place. NIV

Devotional Reflection

It is possible to do many things right and still lose your first love. Jesus' words to the church reveal that spiritual activity cannot replace affection. Our devotion requires vigilance and awareness. A fearful or cooling heart rarely happens suddenly. It typically cools through repeated neglect.

The remedy Jesus offers is not condemnation, but an invitation to return, remember, repent, and renew. Affection can be restored and love can be rekindled. God does not abandon a drifting heart, rather He invites it back.

This discipleship prayer becomes a safeguard. It is a daily request that keeps love alive and faith real, not mechanical.

Life Implications

A vigilant disciple will attend to affection as carefully as belief. Love is sustained through intentional focus rather than assumed endurance. Small acts of remembrance and renewal protect the heart from gradual drift. The target of this prayer is not constant intensity but consistent attentiveness. Jesus wants a life that values ongoing renewal and guards the central reality of love. That requires intentionality.

Reflection Questions

1. Have I noticed signs of spiritual coldness in my life?

2. What can help me return to genuine love for Christ?

Daily Prayer

Lord, guard my heart from growing cold, and continually renew my love for You, Your Word, and Your will.

Notes

Section 2 — Reflection Summary
Growing Affection for Jesus, His Word, and His Will

This section has focused on desire not on effort. It recognizes that discipleship is sustained not merely by discipline, but by affection—by what the heart is drawn toward over time. Love for Jesus, delight in His Word, and trust in His will cannot be assumed, they must be cultivated.

Affection fades when attention drifts because faith can still be active even while desire grows thin. This section acknowledges reality without judgment and invites honesty rather than performance. The prayer to "ignite" affection is not a demand for emotional intensity, but a humble request for constant attention. God is not offended by dryness, He meets it with an invitation.

As affection for Jesus deepens obedience becomes less strained. As love for Scripture grows, listening replaces obligation. As trust in God's will increases, resistance gives way to willingness. None of these happen instantly, because affection is formed through attention and repeated focus.

We have been reminded that love for God is not sustained by willpower alone. It grows where space is made, where competing loves are named, and where the heart is gently reoriented toward what truly has meaning.

Rather than asking whether affection feels strong, the better question is whether attention is being given. Desire follows where the heart is allowed to linger.

Reflection

- What competes most consistently for my attention and desire?
- How might making space for God reshape what I want?

My Closing Response

Lord, You know my heart better than I do. Where affection has cooled, gently awaken desire. Where my attention has been scattered, draw it back to You. Teach me to love You—not by effort alone, but through presence, trust, and focus. Ignite in me a deeper affection for You, for Your Word, and for Your will in my life. Amen.

Notes

My Discipleship Life Prayer

Father, make Jesus the central reality of my life:

1) Ignite in me a deep affection for Jesus, Your Word, and Your will in my life.
2) **Fill my heart and mind with Your presence, power, wisdom, and love, in order that I might abide in You, so I can love You with all my heart, mind, body, and soul, and love my neighbor as I love myself.**
3) Thank you for Your grace, sacrifice, forgiveness, and the gift of salvation that allows me to live confidently in the family of God.
4) Give me knowledge, understanding, and wisdom to make godly decisions, living in humble obedience to Your ways.
5) Give me strength, patience, and perseverance to reject the foolish values of this world, in order to love and worship You all the days of my life.
6) Produce spiritual fruit in me: love, joy, peace, patience, kindness, goodness, faithfulness, gentleness, and self-control so that I can live and walk by the Spirit, rejecting the sins of my flesh.
7) Allow my words and actions to help others believe the Gospel, drawing them to Christ.
8) Empower me to be bold, stand firm, walk faithfully, and endure all adversity to bring glory to Your Name.
9) Help me to be grateful and satisfied with whatever I have.
10) Lord, I surrender myself fully to You. Please create in me a clean heart, and renew a right and steadfast spirit within me.

Lord, heap blessing on me and my family today; bring peace, contentment, and rest into our lives and homes in order that our faithful service brings glory and honor to Your Name. Amen.

SECTION 3

Abiding in God to Love Fully

Prayer Focus:

"Fill my heart and mind with Your presence, power, wisdom, and love, in order that I might abide in You, so I can love You with all my heart, mind, body, and soul, and love my neighbor as I love myself."

Day 11
Abiding, Not Striving

Discipleship Life Prayer Focus
"Fill my heart and mind with Your presence."

John 15:4–5 Abide in me, and I in you. As the branch cannot bear fruit by itself, unless it abides in the vine, neither can you, unless you abide in me. I am the vine; you are the branches. Whoever abides in me and I in him, he it is that bears much fruit, for apart from me you can do nothing. ESV

Devotional Reflection

Many believers live as if spiritual growth depends primarily on effort. Jesus offers a different way. He invites His followers not to work harder, but to abide—to remain connected to Him as a branch remains connected to the vine. Life and fruitfulness flow from a connection to Jesus.

This discipleship prayer recognizes that without Christ, even sincere effort produces little lasting good. Abiding is a posture of dependence. It means choosing closeness over control and presence over performance. When we abide, God supplies what we lack: strength, wisdom, patience, and love.

Abiding does not remove responsibility, but it changes the source of power. We obey Him because of our relationship rather than rules. Abiding reshapes how we approach every part of life.

Life Implications

A life formed by abiding learns to value connection and relationship. Performance gives way to dependence. Productivity is no longer the measure of spiritual health. Attention shifts from managing outcomes to abiding in Christ. When abiding becomes the normal reality, trust and fruitfulness emerge naturally. The result is a life increasingly sustained by relationship. Faith is lived from closeness to Jesus rather than constant activity.

Reflection Questions

1. Where do I tend to perform instead of abide?

2. What can help me stay spiritually attentive and dependent on Him?

Daily Prayer

Father, fill my heart and mind with Your presence and help me abide in You rather than strive for achievement.

Notes

Day 12
Being Filled With God's Presence

Discipleship Life Prayer Focus
"Fill my heart and mind with Your presence, power, wisdom, and love."

Ephesians 3:16–19 I pray that out of his glorious riches he may strengthen you with power through his Spirit in your inner being, so that Christ may dwell in your hearts through faith. And I pray that you, being rooted and established in love, may have power, together with all the Lord's holy people, to grasp how wide and long and high and deep is the love of Christ, and to know this love that surpasses knowledge – that you may be filled to the measure of all the fullness of God. NIV

Devotional Reflection

This prayer asks God for guidance and fullness. It recognizes that the heart and mind are always being filled by something: fear, distraction, ambition, or peace. The question is not *whether* something fills us, but *what* fills us.

God's presence brings strength that overcomes weakness and wisdom that clarifies confusion. His love anchors our soul. When God fills the inner life, external pressures lose their dominance. We are able to respond rather than react.

Being filled with God's presence is not a one-time experience, it is a daily invitation. Each day we open our hearts to Him, trusting God to supply what we cannot generate ourselves.

Life Implications

A life continually filled with God's presence becomes steadier and less reactive. Inner peace replaces anxiety-driven performance and clarity emerges amid confusion. When God's presence shapes the heart and mind, responses become more measured and grounded in confident assurance. The request of this prayer is not emotional intensity, but quiet stability. The goal is a life increasingly governed by God's wisdom and love.

Reflection Questions

1. What most frequently fills my heart and mind throughout the day?

2. How can I make room for God's presence more intentionally?

Daily Prayer

Father, fill my heart and mind with Your presence, power, wisdom, and love today.

Notes

Day 13
Loving God With Your Whole Being

Discipleship Life Prayer Focus

"So I can love You with all my heart, mind, body, and soul."

Mark 12:29–30 "The most important one, answered Jesus, is this: 'Hear, O Israel: the Lord our God, the Lord is one. Love the Lord your God with all your heart and with all your soul and with all your mind and with all your strength.'" NIV

Devotional Reflection

Jesus described love for God as total and integrated. Faith is not confined to thoughts or feelings, because it involves the whole person. This prayer invites a unified life, in which belief, desire, and action move in the same direction.

Loving God with heart, mind, body, and soul means allowing faith to shape our thoughts, habits, priorities, and responses. God is honored not only in spiritual moments, but in ordinary ones: during work or rest, in decisions, relationships, and generally in all ways.

This prayer invites wholeness. When love for God touches every part of life, faith becomes coherent and deeply rooted in the Divine.

Life Implications

Wholehearted love forms an integrated faith life. Faith will shape thoughts, habits, and physical rhythms. When love for God touches every part of life, alignment with Him replaces fragmentation. The goal is not perfection, but alignment—a life increasingly unified in purpose with God. Belief and practice move in the same direction under God's authority.

Reflection Questions

1. Which part of my life is least aligned with loving God with all my heart?

2. What would wholehearted love for God look like in my life?

Daily Prayer

Lord, help me love You with my whole being, uniting my thoughts, actions, and desires in faithful devotion.

Notes

Day 14
Loving Others From God's Overflow

Discipleship Life Prayer Focus
"So I can love my neighbor as I love myself."

1 John 4:19–21 We love because he first loved us. Whoever claims to love God yet hates a brother or sister is a liar. For whoever does not love their brother and.sister, whom they have seen, cannot love God, whom they have not seen. And he has given us this command: anyone who loves God must also love their brother and sister. NIV

Devotional Reflection

Love for others is not sustained by willpower alone. Scripture reminds us that we love because God first loved us. This prayer acknowledges that genuine love flows outward from an inner experience of God's love.

When we are filled with God's presence, patience grows, compassion deepens, and grace becomes more natural. Loving others then becomes an overflow rather than a performance. Without that overflow, love can become strained and mechanical.

This discipleship prayer invites honesty about the limitations and dependence on God's love as the source of real love.

Life Implications

A life rooted in God's love learns to give without depletion. Patience and compassion grow as love flows from fullness rather than obligation. Relationships become less transactional and more gracious.

The result of this prayer is a posture of generosity sustained by God's love—one that allows others to be loved well without exhausting the soul or hardening the heart.

Reflection Questions

1. Where do I find it most difficult to love others well?
2. How might a deeper awareness of God's love change my responses?

Daily Prayer

Father, fill me with Your love so that I may love others from the overflow of Your grace.

Notes

Day 15
Connection: Abiding in Christ

Discipleship Life Prayer Focus
"That I might abide in You."

1 John 3:24 Those who obey his commands live in Him, and he in them. And this is how we know that he lives in us: We know it by the Spirit he gave us. NIV

Devotional Reflection

Abiding in Christ is not limited to prayer or Bible study, but extends into every word spoken and every action taken. Scripture calls believers to do all things in the name of the Lord Jesus, integrating faith with our everyday life.

This prayer invites consistency. It challenges the divide between sacred and ordinary by affirming that Christ's presence belongs in every moment. When faith touches every part of life, even routine tasks gain meaning.

Abiding becomes a way of living a steady, attentive, and God-centered life.

Life Implications

You should recognize Christ's presence in both ordinary and special moments. There is no divide between sacred and daily life. All work and responsibilities are approached with loving attentiveness to Christ.

The result is a life marked by consistency—faith woven quietly and steadily into every part of daily living rather than reserved for spiritual moments or events.

Reflection Questions

1. Where do I tend to separate faith from daily activity?

2. What would help me remain more consciously aware of Christ throughout the day?

Daily Prayer

Lord, help me abide in You throughout every part of my day, in both ordinary and sacred moments.

Notes

Section 3 — Reflection Summary

Abiding in God to Love Fully

This section has drawn attention away from performance and toward abiding. Rather than emphasizing effort, it has explored the sustaining relationship that makes faithful living possible. Abiding is not inactivity, it is intentional dependence. It recognizes that spiritual life does not begin with what we do for God, but with remaining connected to Him.

When the heart and mind are filled with God's presence, love is no longer forced or selective. Love for God becomes integrated, touching thoughts, desires, habits, and actions. Love for others then flows from the overflow of that heart of love.

We have challenged the habit of compartmentalizing faith. Loving God with the whole self resists separation between spiritual moments and ordinary life. Abiding invites consistency. It allows Christ's presence to shape work, relationships, and responsibilities. Faith becomes less reactive and more about consistent adherence.

Finally, this section has reminded us that abiding is a way of living. It is not a technique. It is practiced through attentiveness and trust, and by a repeated return to what matters most. When faith touches every part of life, even the ordinary becomes meaningful.

Rather than asking whether life feels spiritually productive, this section invites a quieter question: *Am I remaining connected?* From that connection, love grows naturally and steadily.

Reflection

- Where do I most often slip into striving rather than abiding?
- What helps me remain attentive to God throughout the day?

My Closing Response

God, I acknowledge my limits. I cannot produce lasting love on my own. Teach me to remain in You—to draw life, strength, and direction from Your presence. Let my love for You shape every part of who I am, and let my love for others flow from what You supply. Keep my life grounded in You, day by day.

Notes

My Discipleship Life Prayer

Father, make Jesus the central reality of my life:

1) Ignite in me a deep affection for Jesus, Your Word, and Your will in my life.
2) Fill my heart and mind with Your presence, power, wisdom, and love, in order that I might abide in You, so I can love You with all my heart, mind, body, and soul, and love my neighbor as I love myself.
3) **Thank you for Your grace, sacrifice, forgiveness, and the gift of salvation that allows me to live confidently in the family of God.**
4) Give me knowledge, understanding, and wisdom to make godly decisions, living in humble obedience to Your ways.
5) Give me strength, patience, and perseverance to reject the foolish values of this world, in order to love and worship You all the days of my life.
6) Produce spiritual fruit in me: love, joy, peace, patience, kindness, goodness, faithfulness, gentleness, and self-control so that I can live and walk by the Spirit, rejecting the sins of my flesh.
7) Allow my words and actions to help others believe the Gospel, drawing them to Christ.
8) Empower me to be bold, stand firm, walk faithfully, and endure all adversity to bring glory to Your Name.
9) Help me to be grateful and satisfied with whatever I have.
10) Lord, I surrender myself fully to You. Please create in me a clean heart, and renew a right and steadfast spirit within me.

Lord, heap blessing on me and my family today; bring peace, contentment, and rest into our lives and homes in order that our faithful service brings glory and honor to Your Name. Amen.

SECTION 4

Living Confidently in Grace and Salvation

Prayer Focus:

"Thank you for Your grace, sacrifice, forgiveness, and the gift of salvation that allows me to live confidently in the family of God."

Day 16
Saved by Grace, Not Performance

Discipleship Life Prayer Focus
"Thank You for Your grace and the gift of salvation."

Ephesians 2:8–9 For it is by grace you have been saved, through faith – and this is not from yourselves, it is the gift of God – not by works, so that no one can boast. NIV

Devotional Reflection

The Christian life does not begin with effort, it begins with grace. This prayer reminds us that salvation is not a reward for good behavior or spiritual achievement. It is a gift, freely given by God's grace and mercy. Grace removes the pressure to earn what has already been secured through Christ.

When grace is misunderstood, faith can become exhausting. We strive to prove ourselves worthy, fearing that failure might disqualify us. Scripture speaks directly against this fear. Our salvation rests not on what we have done, but on what Christ has done for us.

We are invited to rest in grace, remembering the true gift He gave us. Obedience still matters, but it flows from gratitude, not obligation. Grace becomes the foundation for growth and service, not an excuse for passivity.

Life Implications

A life grounded in grace learns to rest rather than strive for approval. Performance-driven faith gives way to gratitude-centered obedience. Identity becomes less fragile as personal worth is received from God rather than earned.

The result is a life increasingly freed from fear of failure, where growth flows from assurance and obedience is shaped by gratitude.

Reflection Questions

1. Do I relate to God as someone earning approval or as one receiving grace?

2. How would my faith change if I truly rested in God's gift of salvation?

Daily Prayer

Father, thank You for Your grace and the gift of salvation which You provided through Christ.

Notes

Day 17
Living as God's Child, Not a Guest

Discipleship Life Prayer Focus
"That I might live confidently in the family of God."

Romans 8:15–17 The Spirit you received does not make you slaves, so that you live in fear again; rather, the Spirit you received brought about your adoption to sonship. And by him we cry, 'Abba, Father. 'The Spirit himself testifies with our spirit that we are God's children. Now if we are children, then we are heirs – heirs of God and co-heirs with Christ, if indeed we share in his sufferings in order that we may also share in his glory. NIV

Devotional Reflection

Salvation brings more than forgiveness: it brings belonging. Scripture describes believers as part of the family of God, not as visitors in God's house. This devotional prayer invites us to move from spiritual insecurity to confident relationship.

Many live as though they must constantly prove they belong. Fear of rejection can shape prayer, obedience, service, worship, and self-perception. Yet God's Spirit affirms our identity as sons and daughters. Confidence in belonging to God's family should produce peace not breed arrogance.

We are invited to shift from a guarded faith to relational trust. A member of His family has confidence to approach God freely and humbly respond to correction. This allows us to walk with Him in greater assurance.

Life Implications

A life rooted in relationship grows in confidence and peace. Insecurity loosens its grip as our identity in Christ is anchored in the knowledge of adoption rather than achievement. Prayer becomes more honest and obedience more relaxed. It is sincere.

The eternal hope of this prayer is a life marked by relational trust. It is one that approaches God freely while responding humbly to correction. We live in the assurance of being fully welcomed into God's family.

Reflection Questions

1. Do I live as someone who already belongs to God, or someone trying to earn a place?
2. How does knowing I am in the family of God shape my daily confidence?

Daily Prayer

Father, thank You that I belong to You as Your child and have been welcomed fully into the family of God.

Notes

Day 18
Freedom From Guilt and Shame

Discipleship Life Prayer Focus
"Thank You for Your forgiveness."

Romans 8:1 Therefore, there is now no condemnation for those who are in Christ Jesus. NIV

Devotional Reflection

Forgiveness removes guilt and grace dissolves shame. Scripture declares that there is no condemnation for those who are in Christ Jesus. Yet many believers continue to live under the weight of past failures, allowing shame to shape their identity and distance them from God.

Forgiveness does not deny sin; rather it overcomes it. God's grace accounts for failure without defining us by it. Shame may indicate a deeper struggle to trust God's total and complete forgiveness.

We have freedom to forget the past and stop living under its control. Grace restores relationship with Him and renews our hope. He is a God who forgives and welcomes us back into relationship with Him.

Life Implications

A life shaped by forgiveness gradually releases the weight of the past. Guilt no longer defines identity and shame loses its power to distance our heart from God. Grace creates space for honesty without fear and repentance without despair.

The result of this prayer is a life increasingly marked by freedom, one that lives and moves forward with humility and hope. The burden of condemnation has been replaced by Christ's sacrifice.

Reflection Questions

1. What past failures still influence how I see myself?

2. How might trusting God's forgiveness bring greater freedom today?

Daily Prayer

Father, thank You for Your forgiveness and for freeing me from guilt and condemnation.

Notes

Day 19
Confidence Rooted in Christ's Sacrifice

Discipleship Life Prayer Focus

"Thank You for Your sacrifice."

Hebrews 10:19–22 Therefore, brothers and sisters, since we have confidence to enter the Most Holy Place by the blood of Jesus, by a new and living way opened for us through the curtain, that is, his body, and since we have a great priest over the house of God, let us draw near to God with a sincere heart and with the full assurance that faith brings, having our hearts sprinkled to cleanse us from a guilty conscience and having our bodies washed with pure water. NIV

Devotional Reflection

Christian confidence does not come from moral strength or spiritual consistency; it comes from Christ's sacrifice. Scripture teaches that believers can approach God with confidence because Jesus has opened the way to a loving relationship. This reminds us that access to God is secure. It is not tentative.

When confidence is misplaced, faith can become fragile. Prayer can be honest and bold when faith is rooted in Christ's finished work. We come to God not because we are strong but because He is faithful.

This prayer provides assurance grounded in Christ alone. Jesus' love and care is always steady and secure.

Life Implications

A life anchored in Christ's sacrifice develops steady confidence and assurance. Our confidence becomes less dependent on consistency or strength and more rooted in what Christ has already accomplished. Prayer grows bolder and more honest, shaped by trust rather than self-evaluation. The hope of this prayer is for a life that approaches God with confidence, grounded in grace rather than self-reliance.

Reflection Questions

1. What do I rely on most for my spiritual confidence?

2. Does Christ's sacrifice change how I approach God?

Daily Prayer

Lord Jesus, thank You for Your sacrifice that gives me confident access to God.

Notes

Day 20
Grace That Shapes How We Live

Discipleship Life Prayer Focus
"Thank You for the grace that allows me to live confidently."

Titus 2:11–12 For the grace of God has appeared that offers salvation to all people. It teaches us to say 'No' to ungodliness and worldly passions, and to live self-controlled, upright and godly lives in this present age. NIV

Devotional Reflection

Grace does more than forgive: it transforms. Scripture teaches that grace instructs us to live wise, self-controlled, gentle, and godly lives. Titus challenges the idea that grace excuses complacency. True grace should reshape our desire for God and strengthen our obedience.

When grace is rightly understood and accepted it motivates change without fear. It teaches us to say "no" to what destroys and "yes" to what gives life. Confidence in grace leads to intentional discipleship.

This prayer encourages a life shaped by gratitude and guided by God's transforming grace.

Life Implications

A life formed by grace grows intentionally rather than passively. Grace reshapes our desires, teaching the heart to value what leads to life. Obedience becomes purposeful and hopeful rather than feeling forced.

The result is a life increasingly guided by gratitude that responds to grace and thoughtful living. It will be shaped by trust in God's transforming work in our lives.

Reflection Questions

1. How has grace influenced the way I live?

2. Is God's grace calling me to grow or change?

Daily Prayer

Father, thank You for the grace that shapes my life and leads me into confident obedience to Your ways.

Notes

Section 4 — Reflection Summary
Living Confidently in Grace and Salvation

This week we focused on the foundation of Christian confidence: grace received, not performance. Rather than emphasizing effort or consistency, it has returned repeatedly to what has already been secured through Christ. Salvation and forgiveness are not fragile. They rest on God's grace.

Grace reshapes how faith is lived. When confidence is rooted in Christ's sacrifice rather than personal success, fear loosens its grip. Guilt and shame should not define our identity. Obedience becomes a response of gratitude instead of an attempt to earn approval. This reminds us that living confidently in the family of God does not produce arrogance, but peace and humility.

Identity as God's child comes before growth in godliness. When this order is reversed, faith can become exhausting. When it is rightly ordered, grace becomes the soil in which transformation takes place. God's forgiveness does not minimize sin, but it does remove condemnation. His grace empowers change.

We have emphasized that grace is active. It teaches, shapes, and guides. Confidence in salvation leads to a life increasingly aligned with God's ways , not to complacency. Thus, grace becomes not only the entry point into faith, but the ongoing strength that sustains it.

Consider not whether you are "doing enough," but whether you are confident in what Christ has already done.

Reflection

- Where do I relate to God in performance rather than grace?
- How does knowing I belong to God's family affect my confidence and peace?

My Closing Response

Father, thank You for Your grace and the gift of salvation. Teach me to live from what has already been given, not from fear or self-effort. Help me rest in forgiveness, walk confidently as Your child, and allow Your grace to shape how I live each day. Allow gratitude to guide my obedience.

Notes

My Discipleship Life Prayer

Father, make Jesus the central reality of my life:

1) Ignite in me a deep affection for Jesus, Your Word, and Your will in my life.
2) Fill my heart and mind with Your presence, power, wisdom, and love, in order that I might abide in You, so I can love You with all my heart, mind, body, and soul, and love my neighbor as I love myself.
3) Thank you for Your grace, sacrifice, forgiveness, and the gift of salvation that allows me to live confidently in the family of God.
4) **Give me knowledge, understanding, and wisdom to make godly decisions, living in humble obedience to Your ways.**
5) Give me strength, patience, and perseverance to reject the foolish values of this world, in order to love and worship You all the days of my life.
6) Produce spiritual fruit in me: love, joy, peace, patience, kindness, goodness, faithfulness, gentleness, and self-control so that I can live and walk by the Spirit, rejecting the sins of my flesh.
7) Allow my words and actions to help others believe the Gospel, drawing them to Christ.
8) Empower me to be bold, stand firm, walk faithfully, and endure all adversity to bring glory to Your Name.
9) Help me to be grateful and satisfied with whatever I have.
10) Lord, I surrender myself fully to You. Please create in me a clean heart, and renew a right and steadfast spirit within me.

Lord, heap blessing on me and my family today; bring peace, contentment, and rest into our lives and homes in order that our faithful service brings glory and honor to Your Name. Amen.

SECTION 5

Wisdom and Humble Obedience

Prayer Focus:

"Give me knowledge, understanding, and wisdom to make godly decisions, living in humble obedience to Your ways."

Day 21
Learning the Shape of Wisdom

Discipleship Life Prayer Focus
"Give me knowledge, understanding, and wisdom."

Proverbs 2:1–6 My son, if you accept my words and store up my commands within you, turning your ear to wisdom and applying your heart to understanding – indeed, if you call out for insight and cry aloud for understanding, and if you look for it as for silver and search for it as for hidden treasure, then you will understand the fear of the LORD and find the knowledge of God. For the LORD gives wisdom; from his mouth come knowledge and understanding. NIV

Devotional Reflection

Scripture speaks of wisdom as something we must seek and acquire. Understanding connects knowledge to wisdom showing us how to live it out. This prayer recognizes that wise living does not happen automatically, but is formed through listening, learning, and seeking God's guidance.

Many struggles arise because of lack of wisdom, not effort. God invites His people to pursue wisdom actively, promising that He is delighted to give it. Wisdom gives perspective before it shapes decisions. It teaches us how to see clearly in order to act confidently.

This prayer invites patience into the learning process. Wisdom grows as we remain teachable, attentive to God's Word, and willing to be shaped His ways.

Life Implications

A life formed by wisdom learns to value discernment over urgency. Clarity replaces haste because decisions are approached with greater attentiveness to God's perspective. Wisdom settles into your life slowly and is buoyed by a desire to learn and grow. It creates patience, restraint, and a teachable spirit. The result of this prayer is not instant certainty, but a steady orientation toward living thoughtfully and faithfully under God's guidance.

Reflection Questions

1. Which do I tend to rely on most: knowledge, understanding, or wisdom?

2. How intentionally am I seeking God's wisdom in my daily life?

Daily Prayer

Father, give me knowledge, understanding, and wisdom, and mold how I see and live each day.

Notes

Day 22
Why Wisdom Begins With Humility

Discipleship Life Prayer Focus
"Give me wisdom to make godly decisions."

Proverbs 3:5–7 Trust in the LORD with all your heart and lean not on your own understanding; in all your ways submit to him, and he will make your paths straight. Do not be wise in your own eyes; fear the LORD and shun evil. NIV

Devotional Reflection

Humility is the doorway to wisdom. Scripture warns that leaning on our own understanding limits what God can do in our lives. Today's devotional helps us recognize how easily confidence becomes self-reliance and how quickly that can dull spiritual discernment.

Humility does not mean indecision or weakness. It means acknowledging limits and welcoming God's direction. Trusting the Lord with all our heart requires surrendering the need to control outcomes or justify preferences.

The prayer asks for wisdom shaped by trust rather than pride. Wisdom listens before acting, and submits to Him before deciding.

Life Implications

Confidence rooted in personal understanding can be replaced by trust in God's direction. Humility disrupts the impulse to control outcomes or defend preferences, creating space for wise discernment. Thus, life is increasingly freed from the burden of self-sufficiency and guided instead by trusting godly wisdom.

Reflection Questions

1. Where do I struggle most to trust God's direction?
2. How does humility or lack thereof, affect my decision-making?

Daily Prayer

Father, teach me humility, that I may trust You fully and receive Your wisdom in every decision.

Notes

Day 23
Asking God for Wisdom Daily

Discipleship Life Prayer Focus
"Give me wisdom to make godly decisions."

James 1:5 If any of you lacks wisdom, you should ask God, who gives generously to all without finding fault, and it will be given to you. NIV

Devotional Reflection

God invites His people to ask for wisdom. Wisdom is not reserved for special moments or spiritual experts, but is available to everyone for daily decisions. James emphasizes God's generosity, assuring us that wisdom is given freely.

Often, decisions are made hastily or anxiously because we forget to ask for God's help. This prayer encourages a slower, more attentive posture; one that pauses to seek God's perspective before moving forward.

Asking for wisdom regularly shapes how we approach life. It cultivates dependence, patience, and clarity.

Life Implications

A life that regularly asks for wisdom will begin to slow its pace. Over time, prayer becomes woven into ordinary decisions rather than reserved for moments of crisis. Discernment settles into daily rhythms so that choices and responses are shaped by attentiveness to God's wisdom.

The result is a life marked by thoughtful dependence, in which seeking God's wisdom becomes a natural part of how decisions are made.

Reflection Questions

1. Do I pause to ask God for wisdom before I make a choice?

2. Which current decision that I have made would benefit from more intentional prayer?

Daily Prayer

Father, I ask You for wisdom today, trusting Your generous guidance in every choice I face.

Notes

Day 24
Obedience as the Fruit of Wisdom

Discipleship Life Prayer Focus
"Living in humble obedience to Your ways."

Deuteronomy 5:33 Walk in obedience to all that the LORD your God has commanded you, so that you may live and prosper and prolong your days in the land that you will possess. NIV

Devotional Reflection

Wisdom and obedience are inseparable. Scripture reminds us that God's ways lead to life, not restriction. Wisdom listens and obedience responds. Knowing what is right is of little value if one refuses to act upon that knowledge.

God's Word challenges the idea that obedience is optional or negotiable. Humble obedience acknowledges that God's ways are better than our instincts. Obedience may not always feel easy or natural, but it produces long-term fruit.

This prayer encourages alignment between understanding and action. Our decisions should produce behavior based on belief and real reliance on His wisdom.

Life Implications

A life guided by wisdom accepts that obedience is not separate from understanding, but the natural result. Alignment with God will replace hesitation as trust in His ways deepens. Obedience becomes less about compliance and more about trusting in His ways.

The result is a life increasingly shaped by faithful responses, where knowing and doing grow together in humility.

Reflection Questions

1. In what areas of my life do I know what God wants but I hesitate to obey?

2. What step of obedience is God inviting me to take?

Daily Prayer

Father, help me live in humble obedience, trusting that Your ways lead to life and blessing.

Notes

Day 25
Trusting God When Choices Are Costly

Discipleship Life Prayer Focus
"Help me make godly decisions."

Isaiah 55:8–9 "For my thoughts are not your thoughts, neither are your ways my ways" declares the LORD."As the heavens are higher than the earth, so are my ways higher than your ways and my thoughts than your thoughts." NIV

Devotional Reflection

Some decisions test trust more than others. God's ways often differ from what feels natural or advantageous. These are the moments when obedience must carry the cost and wisdom require holding to our faith.

God reminds His people that His thoughts are higher and His ways beyond our full understanding. Trusting Him means believing that obedience leads to the right result, even when outcomes are unclear. Choices influenced by God shape our character and deepen dependence on Him.

Thus, we pray for courage to follow God's wisdom, even when it disrupts comfort or personal desires.

Life Implications

This prayer reshapes how cost is understood. Fear of loss gives way to confidence in God's purposes, even when obedience may disrupt our comfort. Trust should resist the impulse to choose what feels safest or most advantageous and confirm our reliance on God.

Thus life becomes more willing to follow God's wisdom with courage, trusting that our faithfulness will lead to a satisfied and grounded life.

Reflection Questions

1. Where am I facing a decision that feels costly, urgent, or uncertain?

2. What would trusting God look like in this situation?

Daily Prayer

Father, give me faith and courage to follow and trust Your wisdom, even when my decisions are costly.

Notes

Section 5 — Reflection Summary

Wisdom and Humble Obedience

This section has explored wisdom as a way of living guided by trust, humility, and obedience. Scripture presents wisdom as something God delights to give, yet it must be sought with openness and patience. Knowledge and understanding inform decisions, but wisdom ultimately guides how truth should be lived out in real situations.

A recurring theme in this section has been humility. Wisdom begins where self-reliance ends. Trusting God with the heart, rather than leaning solely on personal insight, creates space for discernment that goes beyond personal preference or impulse. Humility does not weaken decision-making, but steadies it by acknowledging limits and welcoming God's direction.

We have emphasized that wisdom and obedience belong together. Insight without action is incomplete. Obedience is not blind compliance, but a response grounded in confidence that God's ways lead to life. Even when choices are unclear, trusting God's wisdom forms character and deepens dependence on Him.

This section has reminded us that wise living is developed over time. Decisions shape habits and habits shape character. Wisdom grows through daily seeking, prayerful waiting, and courage to obey, even when the outcomes are difficult.

The challenge is not knowing every decision feels clear, but whether our posture is teachable and willing to follow God's lead.

Reflection

- Where do I rely on my own understanding rather than God's?
- How has humility shaped my recent decisions?
- What step of obedience is God inviting me to take?

My Closing Response

Lord, You are the source of all true wisdom. Teach me to seek Your understanding above my own, to listen before deciding, and to trust Your ways even when they challenge my preferences. Give me a humble heart that is willing to obey, and shape my life through choices that honor You.

Notes

My Discipleship Life Prayer

Father, make Jesus the central reality of my life:

1) Ignite in me a deep affection for Jesus, Your Word, and Your will in my life.
2) Fill my heart and mind with Your presence, power, wisdom, and love, in order that I might abide in You, so I can love You with all my heart, mind, body, and soul, and love my neighbor as I love myself.
3) Thank you for Your grace, sacrifice, forgiveness, and the gift of salvation that allows me to live confidently in the family of God.
4) Give me knowledge, understanding, and wisdom to make godly decisions, living in humble obedience to Your ways.
5) **Give me strength, patience, and perseverance to reject the foolish values of this world, in order to love and worship You all the days of my life.**
6) Produce spiritual fruit in me: love, joy, peace, patience, kindness, goodness, faithfulness, gentleness, and self-control so that I can live and walk by the Spirit, rejecting the sins of my flesh.
7) Allow my words and actions to help others believe the Gospel, drawing them to Christ.
8) Empower me to be bold, stand firm, walk faithfully, and endure all adversity to bring glory to Your Name.
9) Help me to be grateful and satisfied with whatever I have.
10) Lord, I surrender myself fully to You. Please create in me a clean heart, and renew a right and steadfast spirit within me.

Lord, heap blessing on me and my family today; bring peace, contentment, and rest into our lives and homes in order that our faithful service brings glory and honor to Your Name. Amen.

SECTION 6

Rejecting Worldly Values and Choosing Faithful Devotion

Prayer Focus:

**"Give me strength, patience,
and perseverance to reject the
foolish values of this world,
in order to love and worship You,
all the days of my life."**

Day 26
Recognizing the World's Value System

Discipleship Life Prayer Focus

"Give me strength to reject the foolish values of this world."

1 John 2:15–17 Do not love the world or anything in the world. If anyone loves the world, love for the Father is not in them. For everything in the world – the lust of the flesh, the lust of the eyes, and the pride of life – comes not from the Father but from the world. The world and its desires pass away, but whoever does the will of God lives forever. NIV

Devotional Reflection

The world constantly promotes a value system that measures life by success, status, and control. Scripture does not deny the appeal of these things, but it exposes their limits. What the world and its values prize the most is often both temporary and ultimately unsatisfying.

This prayer begins with awareness. Before values can be rejected, they must be recognized. Many of the world's influences are subtle because they quietly shape expectations and priorities. Without discernment they become normal rather than questionable.

God invites His followers to live differently, because His ways lead to life. This prayer asks for clarity to know what truly matters most.

Life Implications

A life shaped by discernment learns to evaluate values rather than absorb them. With time awareness replaces assumption and the heart becomes more attentive to what truly determines priorities. When God's perspective is given greater weight, temporary measures of success lose their authority.

The result is that a life increasingly oriented toward what endures will be guided by wisdom rather than worldly values.

Reflection Questions

1. Which worldly values most influence my thinking or priorities?

2. How do I discern between what is culturally promoted and spiritually wise?

Daily Prayer

Father, give me strength and clarity to recognize and reject values that draw my heart away from You.

Notes

Day 27
Choosing Faithfulness Over Popularity

Discipleship Life Prayer Focus
"Give me perseverance to reject the foolish values of this world."

Romans 12:1–2 Therefore, I urge you, brothers and sisters, in view of God's mercy, to offer your bodies as a living sacrifice, holy and pleasing to God – this is your true and proper worship. Do not conform to the pattern of this world, but be transformed by the renewing of your mind. Then you will be able to test and approve what God's will is – his good, pleasing and perfect will. NIV

Devotional Reflection

Faithfulness often requires resisting pressure to conform. Scripture calls believers to be transformed rather than shaped by the values around them. In today's culture choosing God's ways can feel isolating or be misunderstood.

Popularity promises acceptance, but faithfulness offers transformation. When we conform to the world, faith loses its importance. When we resist the world, obedience becomes an act of worship. This prayer invites us to display courage in order to live life intentionally guided by God's truth.

Faithfulness may not always be noticed by the world, but it's always seen by God.

Life Implications

This prayer resists the pull of conformity. The desire for approval loosens its hold, making room for conviction shaped by God's truth. Faithfulness disrupts the impulse to measure worth by acceptance or recognition. The focus of this prayer is a life governed less by external pressure and more in obedience.

Reflection Questions

1. Where do I feel pressure to conform rather than remain faithful?

2. What would choosing obedience over approval look like for me today?

Daily Prayer

Father, strengthen me to choose faithfulness over popularity and to live guided by Your truth.

Notes

Day 28
Patience in Long Obedience

Discipleship Life Prayer Focus

"Give me patience to love and worship You all my days."

Hebrews 10:36 You need to persevere so that when you have done the will of God, you will receive what he has promised. NIV

Devotional Reflection

Faithful living is not measured by short bursts of commitment but by long-term obedience. This may require temporary patience or long-term perseverance. Scripture reminds us that endurance is necessary to receive what God has promised. We are warned about weariness that can arise when obedience feels unrewarded.

Patience sustains faith when results are delayed. It allows trust to deepen beyond the immediate circumstances. This prayer invites patience in order to remain faithful, even when progress is not visible.

God values perseverance. He works daily shaping character in ways that quick results cannot.

Life Implications

Living a life marked by patience teaches us to remain faithful without constant reinforcement. Endurance settles into daily rhythms—showing up, continuing, and trusting God's work beyond immediate results. Obedience becomes an automatic habit rather than a response to visible reward.

The result is a life of steady perseverance which is sustained by trust rather than urgency.

Reflection Questions

1. When do I feel impatient with God's timing?

2. Where can I practice faithful patience in my current season?

Daily Prayer

Lord, give me patience to remain faithful, trusting Your work even when I cannot see it.

Notes

Day 29
Persevering When Faith Is Tested

Discipleship Life Prayer Focus
"Give me perseverance to remain faithful."

James 1:12 Blessed is the one who perseveres under trial because, having stood the test, that person will receive the crown of life that the Lord has promised to those who love him. NIV

Devotional Reflection

Testing reveals where faith is anchored. Scripture promises blessing to those who endure because it produces depth and maturity, not because endurance is easy. There is often a temptation to retreat when faith becomes difficult.

Perseverance does not deny hardship; rather it chooses trust to combat apathy. This prayer invites strength to remain faithful through dependence on God's sustaining grace, not by our willpower alone.

God does not waste trials. He uses them to refine faith and strengthen hope.

Life Implications

A persevering life develops resilience rooted in trust. Trials are no longer seen just as obstacles, but as places where faith is clarified and strengthened. Endurance shapes perspective, helping the heart remain anchored even when circumstances are difficult.

Thus, life is oriented toward faithfulness that remains steadfast through testing. The faithful are confident that God is at work beyond what is obviously visible.

Reflection Questions

1. How do I usually respond when my faith is tested?

2. What helps me remain faithful during challenging seasons and times?

Daily Prayer

Father, give me perseverance to remain faithful when my faith is tested and trials press in.

Notes

Day 30
Worship as a Lifelong Commitment

Discipleship Life Prayer Focus
"To love and worship You all the days of my life."

Joshua 24:15 But if serving the LORD seems undesirable to you, then choose for yourselves this day whom you will serve, whether the gods your ancestors served beyond the Euphrates, or the gods of the Amorites, in whose land you are living. But as for me and my household, we will serve the LORD. NIV

Devotional Reflection

Worship lasts more than a moment; it is a lifelong orientation of the heart. Joshua's declaration reminds us that serving the Lord is a daily choice, renewed again and again. We are encouraged to experience worship as a way of life.

True worship shapes decisions, priorities, and values. Loving and worshiping God daily requires intentional commitment, especially in a world filled with competing loyalties.

This prayer affirms a settled decision to serve the Lord faithfully, not occasionally, but all the days of your life.

Life Implications

We must challenge the tendency to treat worship as something occasional rather than ongoing and defining. Divided loyalties can give way to settled devotion when daily choices reflect what the heart truly values. Worship must be integrated into our faith practice, calling the whole of our faith life into alignment.

The result is a life increasingly shaped by faithful devotion. It is one that consistently chooses God's ways over competing claims and desires.

Reflection Questions

1. How does my daily life reflect worship beyond the formal practices?

2. What helps me renew my commitment to worship God consistently?

Daily Prayer

Lord, I choose to love and worship You each day, committing my life to faithful devotion.

Notes

Section 6 — Reflection Summary

Rejecting Worldly Values vs Choosing Faithful Devotion

This section has invited careful discernment about the values that shape our daily life. Rather than presenting a dramatic contrast between faith and the world, it has exposed subtle influences. There are assumptions about success, comfort, recognition, and control that can gradually displace wholehearted devotion to God. Recognizing these influences is the first step toward faithful resistance.

A consistent emphasis has been on endurance. Devotion is not sustained through intensity alone, but through perseverance. Choosing God's ways often involves resisting pressure to conform in order to remain patient when answers are slow in coming. It is important to continue to worship even when the desired results are not immediately visible. Obedient choices shape a steady durable faith.

This section has reframed worship as a lifelong experience rather than an occasional practice. Loving and worshiping God "all the days of my life" is expressed through repeated decisions to remain faithful, especially when alternatives promise ease or approval. Devotion deepens through long obedience consistent with God's ways, not through dramatic moments.

Consider how intentional you have you been in choosing what truly matters. Devotion to the Lord grows where discernment and perseverance are practiced together.

Reflection

- Which cultural values most subtly influence my priorities?
- Do I feel pressure to conform rather than remain faithful?
- How can I cultivate patient, long-term devotion, rather than short bursts of commitment?

My Closing Response

God, help me see clearly what shapes my heart and choices. Give me strength to reject values that draw me away from You, and patience to remain faithful. Teach me to love and worship You choosing devotion that endures rather than convenience that fades.

Notes

My Discipleship Life Prayer

Father, make Jesus the central reality of my life:

1) Ignite in me a deep affection for Jesus, Your Word, and Your will in my life.
2) Fill my heart and mind with Your presence, power, wisdom, and love, in order that I might abide in You, so I can love You with all my heart, mind, body, and soul, and love my neighbor as I love myself.
3) Thank you for Your grace, sacrifice, forgiveness, and the gift of salvation that allows me to live confidently in the family of God.
4) Give me knowledge, understanding, and wisdom to make godly decisions, living in humble obedience to Your ways.
5) Give me strength, patience, and perseverance to reject the foolish values of this world, in order to love and worship You all the days of my life.
6) **Produce spiritual fruit in me: love, joy, peace, patience, kindness, goodness, faithfulness, gentleness, and self-control so that I can live and walk by the Spirit, rejecting the sins of my flesh.**
7) Allow my words and actions to help others believe the Gospel, drawing them to Christ.
8) Empower me to be bold, stand firm, walk faithfully, and endure all adversity to bring glory to Your Name.
9) Help me to be grateful and satisfied with whatever I have.
10) Lord, I surrender myself fully to You. Please create in me a clean heart, and renew a right and steadfast spirit within me.

Lord, heap blessing on me and my family today; bring peace, contentment, and rest into our lives and homes in order that our faithful service brings glory and honor to Your Name. Amen.

SECTION 7

Bearing the Fruit of the Spirit

Prayer Focus:

"Produce spiritual fruit in me: love, joy, peace, patience, kindness, goodness, faithfulness, gentleness, and self-control so that I can live and walk by the Spirit, rejecting the sins of my flesh."

Day 31
Fruit That Comes From the Spirit

Discipleship Life Prayer Focus
"Produce spiritual fruit in me."

Galatians 5:22–23 But the fruit of the Spirit is love, joy, peace, forbearance, kindness, goodness, faithfulness, gentleness and self-control. Against such things there is no law. NIV

Devotional Reflection

Spiritual fruit is not the result of self-effort; it is the outcome of a life yielded to God's Spirit. Scripture describes fruit as something produced. This devotional invites us to stop measuring spiritual growth by performance but to look instead at what is forming and driving our inner spirit.

Love, joy, peace, patience, kindness, goodness, faithfulness, gentleness, and self-control reflect the character of Christ lived out in ordinary life. These qualities grow where the Spirit is welcomed and trusted. They develop gradually, often unnoticed, yet they reveal deep transformation.

This discipleship prayer asks God to shape who we are, not just what we do. Spiritual fruit is evidence of connection, not our performance.

Life Implications

A life shaped by the Spirit of God learns to measure growth by character rather than activity. Attention shifts from external productivity to inner transformation. Spiritual health is recognized by the qualities being cultivated in our lives. Fruit develops while life is steadily reflecting Christ's character, which is increasingly oriented toward personal inward growth. We trust the Spirit to produce lasting change beyond what our effort alone can achieve.

Reflection Questions

1. Which fruit of the Spirit do I most desire to exhibit?
2. Am I making space for the Spirit's work in my life?

Daily Prayer

Father, produce spiritual fruit in me as I yield my life to Your influence.

Notes

Day 32
Walking by the Spirit Daily

Discipleship Life Prayer Focus
"So that I can live and walk by the Spirit."

Galatians 5:16 So I say, live by the Spirit, and you will not gratify the desires of the flesh. NIV

Devotional Reflection

Walking by the Spirit describes a daily, moment-by-moment dependence on God's guidance. It is not a dramatic experience reserved for special occasions. Rather it is a steady attentiveness to God's guidance in ordinary moments.

We should be cultivating our awareness of the Spirit. Walking by the Spirit means paying attention to inner promptings, Scripture-shaped convictions, and God's gentle urging. It requires slowing down enough to listen and trusting enough to respond obediently.

Our spiritual life is relational. We are to walk with and abide in God.

Life Implications

We must resist the tendency to rely on habit or self-direction. Dependence on the Spirit replaces automatic responses generated by impulse or routine. Walking by the Spirit disrupts self-sufficiency, inviting attentiveness and trust in God's guidance on a consistent basis.

The result is a life governed by relational awareness. We learn to move through each day with sensitivity to God's leading, rather than our normal default patterns.

Reflection Questions

1. What helps me remain attentive to Jesus and the Spirit's leading?

2. Where do I tend to rely on habits rather than dependence on God?

Daily Prayer

Lord, help me walk by Your Spirit today, attentive and responsive to Your leading.

Notes

Day 33
Replace the Flesh With New Life

Discipleship Life Prayer Focus

"Rejecting the sins of my flesh."

Romans 8:5–6 Those who live according to the flesh have their minds set on what the flesh desires; but those who live in accordance with the Spirit have their minds set on what the Spirit desires. The mind governed by the flesh is death, but the mind governed by the Spirit is life and peace. NIV

Devotional Reflection

Scripture contrasts life shaped by the flesh versus life defined by the Spirit. Scripture addresses the inner conflict believers experience between old patterns and new desires. Rejecting the flesh is not only about avoidance, but also about redirection.

When the mind is set on the Spirit, peace grows. This prayer invites us to replace destructive habits with Spirit-led practices. Growing and living in the Spirit is not only stopping what is wrong, but nurturing what is right.

God's Spirit empowers change where willpower alone fails.

Life Implications

A believer focused on the Spirit learns to redirect desire rather than simply suppress behavior. New patterns are formed as Spirit-led practices take the place of old habits. Transformation occurs daily encouraged by how thoughts are entertained, responses are shaped, and discipline is practiced.

The goal is a life increasingly marked by peace and clarity, where new life grows steadily through intentional Spirit-guided obedience.

Reflection Questions

1. What existing patterns in my life compete with spiritual growth?
2. What Spirit-led habit could replace them?

Daily Prayer

Father, help me set my mind on the Spirit and replace old patterns with new life.

Notes

Day 34
Visible Evidence of Inner Change

Discipleship Life Prayer Focus
"That my life would reflect spiritual fruit."

Matthew 7:16–20 By their fruit you will recognize them. Do people pick grapes from thorn-bushes, or figs from thistles? Likewise, every good tree bears good fruit, but a bad tree bears bad fruit. A good tree cannot bear bad fruit, and a bad tree cannot bear good fruit. Every tree that does not bear good fruit is cut down and thrown into the fire. Thus, by their fruit you will recognize them. NIV

Devotional Reflection

Jesus taught that fruit reveals the nature and value of the tree. Spiritual fruit is revealed through our words and actions, as well as our relationships. We must always be aware what others perceived and experience by observing our lives.

Fruit grows naturally from a good foundation and regular cultivation. When the Spirit works within us, transformation becomes evident to others. This discipleship prayer asks God to make inner change visible, not only for recognition by others but for authenticity and service to others.

Consistency matters more than intensity. Small steady changes reflect the lasting work of the Spirit.

Life Implications

A life formed by the Spirit becomes increasingly authentic. Inner transformation will express itself outwardly through consistent attitudes and actions. Fruit becomes visible through sustained caring and integrity. The result is a life oriented toward authenticity, where inner change and outward expression align naturally and faithfully.

Reflection Questions

1. What spiritual fruit is visible in my life right now?
2. How might God be shaping my character through everyday interactions?

Daily Prayer

Lord, let the work You are doing within me be reflected in visible spiritual fruit.

Notes

Day 35
Growing Slowly but Surely

Discipleship Life Prayer Focus
"Produce spiritual fruit in me."

Philippians 1:6 . . . being confident of this, that he who began a good work in you will carry it on to completion until the day of Christ Jesus. NIV

Devotional Reflection

Spiritual growth often seems slow. This Scripture reminds us that God's work unfolds over time. Scripture assures us that God completes what He begins. Fruit can grow quietly, often beneath the surface, before it becomes visible to others.

This prayer encourages patience because growth is rarely linear. Seasons of pruning, waiting, and endurance prepare the way for deeper fruitfulness. Trusting God's process and timing will guard against discouragement.

God is faithful and He will continue His work even when progress feels slow or unseen.

Life Implications

This prayer challenges impatience with God's pace of transformation. The desire for immediate results is replaced by trust in God's ongoing work. Spiritual growth will resist discouragement, reminding the heart that change will unfold gradually and faithfully.

This prayer is focused on a life freed from measuring progress by time, choosing instead to rest in God's commitment to complete what He has begun through a steady pace and His enduring grace.

Reflection Questions

1. Do I feel discouraged about my spiritual growth?

2. How would trusting God's faithfulness change my focus and perspective?

Daily Prayer

Father, help me trust Your faithful work in me, even when growth feels slow or is unseen.

Notes

Section 7 — Reflection Summary
Bearing the Fruit of the Spirit

This section shifted attention from outward effort to inward formation. Rather than focusing on what must be accomplished, it has emphasized what is being produced through life in the Spirit. Spiritual fruit is not manufactured through discipline alone. It grows where there is dependence and connection with God.

A central theme throughout these days has been patience with the process of growth. Fruit develops gradually, often beneath the surface, before it becomes visible. We are reminded that transformation is not measured by intensity, but by attention, focus, and consistency. Love, joy, peace, and the other qualities of the Spirit emerge where life is being shaped from the inside out.

We have addressed the tension between old patterns and new life. Walking by the Spirit involves redirection as much as resistance—learning to replace what diminishes life with habits that nurture it. The Spirit reshapes will desire and responses, forming character in ways that our effort alone cannot sustain.

Finally, this section has affirmed that visible change matters, not for appearance, but for authenticity. Spiritual fruit becomes evident in relationships, attitudes, and everyday interactions. Growth may feel slow, but God is faithful to complete the work He begins.

As you pause, consider not how quickly change is happening, but whether you are available to the Spirit's shaping work and are trusting Him with the pace of growth.

Reflection

- Which fruit of the Spirit is most needed in my life right now?
- Where do I sense tension between old habits and new desires?

My Closing Response

Holy Spirit, shape my life from the inside out. Produce in me what I cannot create on my own. Teach me to walk with You daily, to release old patterns that hinder growth, and to trust Your steady work within me. Form my character so that my life reflects the life of Christ.

Notes

My Discipleship Life Prayer

Father, make Jesus the central reality of my life:

1) Ignite in me a deep affection for Jesus, Your Word, and Your will in my life.
2) Fill my heart and mind with Your presence, power, wisdom, and love, in order that I might abide in You, so I can love You with all my heart, mind, body, and soul, and love my neighbor as I love myself.
3) Thank you for Your grace, sacrifice, forgiveness, and the gift of salvation that allows me to live confidently in the family of God.
4) Give me knowledge, understanding, and wisdom to make godly decisions, living in humble obedience to Your ways.
5) Give me strength, patience, and perseverance to reject the foolish values of this world, in order to love and worship You all the days of my life.
6) Produce spiritual fruit in me: love, joy, peace, patience, kindness, goodness, faithfulness, gentleness, and self-control so that I can live and walk by the Spirit, rejecting the sins of my flesh.
7) **Allow my words and actions to help others believe the Gospel, drawing them to Christ.**
8) Empower me to be bold, stand firm, walk faithfully, and endure all adversity to bring glory to Your Name.
9) Help me to be grateful and satisfied with whatever I have.
10) Lord, I surrender myself fully to You. Please create in me a clean heart, and renew a right and steadfast spirit within me.

Lord, heap blessing on me and my family today; bring peace, contentment, and rest into our lives and homes in order that our faithful service brings glory and honor to Your Name. Amen.

SECTION 8

Living as a Witness Through Words and Actions

Prayer Focus:

"Allow my words and actions to help others believe the Gospel, drawing them to Christ."

Day 36
Words That Point to Christ

Discipleship Life Prayer Focus
"Allow my words to help others believe the Gospel."

Colossians 4:5–6 Be wise in the way you act towards outsiders; make the most of every opportunity. Let your conversation be always full of grace, seasoned with salt, so that you may know how to answer everyone. NIV

Devotional Reflection

Words carry influence. Scripture reminds us that the way we speak matters, not only what we say, but how we say it. Gracious speech reflects a heart shaped by Christ and invites others to listen rather than withdraw.

We are encouraged to be attentive. Words spoken in patience and humility can open doors that argument never will. God often uses ordinary conversations to plant seeds of truth. This prayer asks for wisdom to speak at the right time, with clarity and kindness.

We are not responsible for convincing others, only for speaking faithfully and lovingly.

Life Implications

A life shaped by Jesus learns to view words as a form of stewardship. Speech becomes more thoughtful and attentive to others, rather than driven by impulse or reaction. Grace begins to guide tone as well as content, creating space for understanding rather than resistance.

The goal of this prayer is a life increasingly oriented toward speaking in ways that reflect Christ's character. Our words should be clothed in wisdom and kindness rather than urgency or bravado.

Reflection Questions

1. How do my words usually affect others? Do they draw them closer or push them away?

2. Can I speak more intentionally today?

Daily Prayer

Father, guide my words today so they reflect Your grace and point others toward Christ.

Notes

Day 37
Actions That Support the Gospel

Discipleship Life Prayer Focus
"Allow my actions to help others believe the Gospel."

Matthew 5:16 In the same way, let your light shine before others, that they may see your good deeds and glorify your Father in heaven. NIV

Devotional Reflection

Jesus taught that visible faith points others toward God. Today's devotional is focused on the power of consistent Christ-like behavior. When faith is lived authentically it becomes credible.

Actions give weight to words. Kindness, integrity, and humility testify to God's work within us. The discipleship prayer asks God to align behavior with belief so that our life becomes a witness to the Truth.

Small acts of faithfulness will leave lasting impressions.

Life Implications

This prayer emphasized the separation between belief and behavior. As time passes, inconsistency loses its hold as daily actions begin to reflect deeply held convictions. Faithfulness should challenge us to speak more, relying on words of truth that proclaim the Gospel.

Life is less fragmented where actions steadily reinforce belief. Credibility will grow through consistent action rather than explanation.

Reflection Questions

1. What do my daily words and actions communicate about my faith?

2. Where might God want me to be more consistent?

Daily Prayer

Lord, align my actions with my faith so that my life reflects the truth of the Gospel.

Notes

Day 38
Integrity in Everyday Life

Discipleship Life Prayer Focus
"Let my life reflect the Gospel."

Titus 2:7–8 In everything set them an example by doing what is good. In your teaching show integrity, seriousness and soundness of speech that cannot be condemned, so that those who oppose you may be ashamed because they have nothing bad to say about us. NIV

Devotional Reflection

Integrity weaves belief and behavior together. Scripture encourages believers to live in a way that cannot easily be dismissed or discredited. Today's scripture passage speaks to the importance of consistency so we are the same person in private as in public.

Integrity does not require perfection; it requires honesty and humility. When mistakes are acknowledged and corrected, faith gains credibility. This prayer invites a life that reflects sincerity rather than one focused on managing one's image.

A life of integrity quietly strengthens your witness.

Life Implications

A life lived with integrity weaves faith into ordinary decisions and routines. Consistency settles into daily life impacting how commitments are kept. It will also guide how mistakes are addressed and responsibility is carried out. Integrity becomes less about image and more about alignment with the truth.

The benefit is a life in which belief and behavior are increasingly consistent, allowing faith to be expressed naturally and credibly through everyday choices.

Reflection Questions

1. Where do I feel tension between what I believe and how I live?
2. Can I pursue greater integrity in ordinary situations?

Daily Prayer

Father, help me live with integrity so that my life reflects the Gospel in every situation.

Notes

Day 39
Faithful Witness in Ordinary Moments

Discipleship Life Prayer Focus

"Use my life to draw others to Christ."

1 Peter 3:15–16 But in your hearts revere Christ as Lord. Always be prepared to give an answer to everyone who asks you to give the reason for the hope that you have. But do this with gentleness and respect, keeping a clear conscience, so that those who speak maliciously against your good behavior in Christ may be ashamed of their slander. NIV

Devotional Reflection

Being a witness is not limited to dramatic moments or formal conversations. Scripture reminds us that everyday faithfulness often speaks the most clearly to the watching world. Gentleness and respect create space for honest dialogue and others curiosity about faith issues.

We are invited to trust in God's timing. Our faithful listening, serving, and responding with grace often will prepare a heart long before words are spoken. This prayer releases pressure to perform and suggests availability instead.

God can work amazing feats through ordinary obedience.

Life Implications

If you are faithful you will value presence over performance. Our witness becomes less about initiative and more about availability. It should cause us to demonstrate patience, listen well, and respond with gentleness. Ordinary moments gain significance as our faith is lived consistently in the shadow of the cross.

The result is a life oriented toward steady faithfulness, trusting God to work through our gentle presence rather than dramatic events.

Reflection Questions

1. Where has God placed me to live faithfully right now?
2. How can I respond to others with greater gentleness and respect?

Daily Prayer

Lord, use my ordinary faithfulness to draw others toward You in Your time.

Notes

Day 40
Trusting God With the Results

Discipleship Life Prayer Focus

"Allow my life to help others believe."

1 Corinthians 3:6–7 I planted the seed, Apollos watered it, but God has been making it grow. So neither the one who plants nor the one who waters is anything, but only God, who makes things grow. NIV

Devotional Reflection

Scripture reminds us that God alone brings growth. Today's devotional addresses the temptation to measure faithfulness by visible results. But our witness should be about respectful, obedience, not outcomes.

This prayer suggests surrender. When we trust God with results, we are freed from pressure and disappointment. Our role is to plant and water faithfully and it is God's role to transform hearts.

Trusting God with the results fosters patience, humility, and peace. We can rest in His ability to complete a good work in us and others.

Life Implications

This prayer loosens the need to control outcomes. Over time, the pressure to measure our impact gives way to trusting in God's work beyond what can be seen. Faithfulness prevents discouragement when results are not what we expected.

The result is a life freed from striving for visible success, one that rests in obedience and allows God to determine growth or transformation according to His purposes and timeframe.

Reflection Questions

1. Where do I feel discouraged by lack of visible results?

2. How can I practice faithful obedience without trying to control outcomes?

Daily Prayer

Father, help me trust You with the results as I live faithfully and obediently before You.

Notes

Section 8 — Reflection Summary
Living as a Witness Through Words and Actions

We have focused on the everyday nature of witness. Rather than emphasizing dramatic moments or persuasive arguments, we have discussed our faith expressed through ordinary words, consistent actions, and a life marked by integrity. Witnessing is not a task to perform but a way of living attentively before others.

A key emphasis throughout this section has been alignment. Words and actions gain credibility when they reflect the same underlying faith. Our spiritual commitment should produce a visible consistent loyalty to Christ without drawing attention to self. We were reminded that such a witness is often shaped through continual faithful presence rather than isolated conversations.

We have also addressed the temptation to measure faithfulness by outcomes. Trusting God with results frees the heart from stress and discouragement. Our role is not to convince or control, but to be faithful, speaking wisely, and allowing God to work beyond what we can see.

Our witness can unfold in ordinary moments: work, family, and community relationships. Gentleness, respect, and patience often speak more clearly than words. A life shaped by Christ becomes its own testimony.

Consider how consistently your life reflects the Gospel in everyday situations, not how visible your witness has been.

Reflection

- How do my words and actions together reflect what I believe?
- How can I put aside my concern over results and focus on being faithful?

My Closing Response

Lord, shape my words and actions so they reflect Your truth. Teach me to speak with grace and live with integrity. Free me from pressure to produce results, and help me trust You with the work only You can do. Use my everyday faithfulness to draw others toward You.

Notes

My Discipleship Life Prayer

Father, make Jesus the central reality of my life:

1) Ignite in me a deep affection for Jesus, Your Word, and Your will in my life.
2) Fill my heart and mind with Your presence, power, wisdom, and love, in order that I might abide in You, so I can love You with all my heart, mind, body, and soul, and love my neighbor as I love myself.
3) Thank you for Your grace, sacrifice, forgiveness, and the gift of salvation that allows me to live confidently in the family of God.
4) Give me knowledge, understanding, and wisdom to make godly decisions, living in humble obedience to Your ways.
5) Give me strength, patience, and perseverance to reject the foolish values of this world, in order to love and worship You all the days of my life.
6) Produce spiritual fruit in me: love, joy, peace, patience, kindness, goodness, faithfulness, gentleness, and self-control so that I can live and walk by the Spirit, rejecting the sins of my flesh.
7) Allow my words and actions to help others believe the Gospel, drawing them to Christ.
8) **Empower me to be bold, stand firm, walk faithfully, and endure all adversity to bring glory to Your Name.**
9) Help me to be grateful and satisfied with whatever I have.
10) Lord, I surrender myself fully to You. Please create in me a clean heart, and renew a right and steadfast spirit within me.

Lord, heap blessing on me and my family today; bring peace, contentment, and rest into our lives and homes in order that our faithful service brings glory and honor to Your Name. Amen.

SECTION 9

Endurance and Courage in Adversity

Prayer Focus:

**"Empower me to be bold,
stand firm, walk faithfully,
and endure all adversity
to bring glory to Your Name."**

Day 41
Boldness Rooted in God's Strength

Discipleship Life Prayer Focus
"Empower me to be bold."

Acts 4:29–31: "Now, Lord, consider their threats and enable your servants to speak your word with great boldness. Stretch out your hand to heal and perform signs and wonders through the name of your holy servant Jesus" After they prayed, the place where they were meeting was shaken. And they were all filled with the Holy Spirit and spoke the word of God boldly. NIV

Devotional Reflection

Boldness in discipleship is not personality-driven confidence, it is courage supplied by God. The early believers prayed for boldness to remain faithful, not about success or safety. Their confidence flowed from trust in God's power rather than control over circumstances.

This Scripture reminds us that fear often silences faith. God's Spirit empowers boldness through the assurance of His presence. When boldness is rooted in God's strength it becomes steady rather than aggressive.

This prayer invites courage grounded in dependence on God, trusting Him to supply what obedience requires.

Life Implications

The believer shaped by God's strength learns to distinguish boldness from bravado. Courage becomes less about personality or confidence and more about reliance on God's power or presence. Fear loses its impact as trust deepens, allowing faith to be expressed calmly and faithfully.

The target is a life increasingly oriented toward obedience rather than self-protection. It is one that draws courage from God's sustaining power rather than from personal control.

Reflection Questions

1. Where do I hesitate to live or speak boldly for Christ?

2. How would reliance on God's strength change my response?

Daily Prayer

Father, empower me with boldness grounded in Your strength and presence.

Notes

Day 42
Standing Firm When Pressured

Discipleship Life Prayer Focus

"Help me stand firm."

1 Corinthians 16:13 Be on your guard; stand firm in the faith; be courageous; be strong. NIV

Devotional Reflection

Standing firm means resistance against compromise. Scripture tells believers to remain alert and grounded when pressure mounts. We acknowledge that faith is often tested through subtle requests to compromise or shade the truth.

Standing firm requires clarity about what matters most. It involves anchoring convictions in truth rather than convenience. This prayer invites resolve driven by trust rather than fear or the desire for results.

Standing firm does not mean rigidity; it means faithfulness under pressure.

Life Implications

This prayer resists the slow drift toward compromise. Pressure to conform loses its power as convictions are clarified and strengthened. Standing firm does not harden the heart, but it does steady it, helping faith remain grounded when convenience or acceptance pulls in another direction.

A disciple will experience a life shaped less by external pressure and more by one anchored in truth. It will be a life of faithfulness without being defensive or rigid.

Reflection Questions

1. Do I feel pressure to compromise my convictions?
2. What truth helps me remain grounded and steadfast in difficult situations?

Daily Prayer

Lord, help me stand firm in faith when pressure to compromise surrounds me.

Notes

Day 43
Walking Faithfully Through Difficulty

Discipleship Life Prayer Focus
"Help me walk faithfully."

2 Corinthians 4:16–18 Therefore we do not lose heart. Though outwardly we are wasting away, yet inwardly we are being renewed day by day. For our light and momentary troubles are achieving for us an eternal glory that far outweighs them all. So we fix our eyes not on what is seen, but on what is unseen, since what is seen is temporary, but what is unseen is eternal. NIV

Devotional Reflection

Faithfulness is often expressed through steady obedience during hardship rather than dramatic victories. Scripture reminds us to look beyond temporary troubles to eternal realities. Disciples may experience seasons when difficulty lingers and answers are delayed. But God is faithful!

Walking faithfully means continuing to trust and obey even when circumstances challenge our hope. This prayer invites perspective, choosing to focus on what is unseen and lasting, rather than on what is worldly and temporary.

God often uses difficulty to refine faith and deepen trust.

Life Implications

The faithful believer will carry trust into hardship without waiting for circumstances to improve. Endurance settles into daily patterns and helps you continue to show up, to pray, and to obey, even when progress is slow. Difficulty becomes part of the growth process rather than a sign of failure.

This prayer seeks a life that integrates faith into hardship, allowing trust to develop responses long before relief arrives.

Reflection Questions

1. What current challenge tests my faith most?
2. How will an eternal perspective reshape my response?

Daily Prayer

Father, help me walk faithfully through difficulty, trusting what You are doing beyond what I can see.

Notes

Day 44
Enduring Without Losing Heart

Discipleship Life Prayer Focus
"Help me endure all adversity."

Galatians 6:9 Let us not become weary in doing good, for at the proper time we will reap a harvest if we do not give up. NIV

Devotional Reflection

Endurance sustains discipleship. Scripture acknowledges weariness and encourages perseverance, reminding us that faithfulness bears fruit according to God's timing. This helps us overcome discouragement that arises when obedience feels challenging.

Enduring does not require ignoring fatigue, but requires trusting God to renew strength. Scripture encourages patience and hope rooted in God's promises rather than in immediate outcomes.

Faithfulness over a lifetime develops our character and a faithful testimony.

Life Implications

A life oriented toward endurance learns to measure faithfulness by perseverance rather than visible results. Discouragement loosens its grip as hope is anchored in God's promises instead of immediate outcomes. Endurance becomes a steady posture, sustained by trust that faithfulness is never wasted.

The implication is a life increasingly marked by resilience; one that continues forward with hope even when encouragement feels scarce.

Reflection Questions

1. When do I feel the most weary in following Christ?

2. What helps me remain faithful when encouragement feels scarce?

Daily Prayer

Lord, strengthen me to endure without losing heart, trusting Your timing and promises.

Notes

Day 45
Living for God's Glory in Hard Seasons

Discipleship Life Prayer Focus

"To bring glory to Your Name."

1 Peter 4:12–13 Dear friends, do not be surprised at the fiery ordeal that has come on you to test you, as though something strange were happening to you. But rejoice inasmuch as you participate in the sufferings of Christ, so that you may be overjoyed when his glory is revealed. NIV

Devotional Reflection

Suffering and adversity do not disqualify faith; in fact, they often refine it. Scripture reminds believers that trials can reveal God's glory through steadfast commitment. This invites reflection on His eternal purposes rather than temporary comfort.

Living for God's glory means we trust Him even when circumstances are difficult. This prayer reorients hardship as opportunity for a deeper witness, not through clarity or argument, but through endurance and joy rooted in Christ.

God's glory is often displayed most clearly in faithful patience or perseverance.

Life Implications

This prayer reframes adversity as being formative. Times of hardship teach us to resist the impulse to retreat into self-pity or resentment. Living for God's glory challenges the assumption that faithfulness depends on ease.

Thus, our life should honor God through perseverance and allow adversity to deepen our witness through steadfast trust, rather than diminish our hope.

Reflection Questions

1. Do I view adversity as interruption or as growth?
2. How could God be glorified and honored through my response to difficulty?

Daily Prayer

Father, help me live for Your glory, trusting You faithfully even in difficult seasons.

Notes

Section 9 — Reflection Summary
Endurance and Courage in Adversity

We have addressed the reality that faithful discipleship is often tested through adversity. Rather than presenting hardship as an interruption to faith, these days have reframed it as a time in which endurance and trust are formed. Boldness, standing firm, and perseverance are not grounded in personal strength, but in reliance on God's sustaining power and presence.

A central emphasis throughout this section has been steadiness. Courage is not portrayed as fearlessness, but as faith expressed in the presence of fear. Endurance is quiet faithfulness maintained during a lifetime. It is not dramatic stubbornness. This section has reminded us that adversity often reveals where faith is anchored and can deepen our trust in what cannot be seen.

We are challenged by the expectation that obedience should be rewarded quickly or visibly. Walking faithfully through difficulty requires an eternal perspective; one that values what God is doing in our circumstances. Endurance becomes an act of hope, trusting that God's purposes extend beyond immediate relief.

We have affirmed that God's glory is not diminished by hardship. In many cases, it is revealed through perseverance, trust, and the quiet joy that remains even when conditions are difficult. Faithfulness during adversity becomes a testimony of hope grounded in Christ Jesus.

As you pause, consider not how quickly most adversity has passed, but how your faith has been shaped while enduring it.

Reflection

- Where is God calling me to courage rather than retreat?
- How do I respond when my faith is tested by difficulty?

My Closing Response

God, strengthen my resolve to remain faithful when life is difficult. Give me courage that rests in You, and endurance that does not lose heart. Help me stand firm, walk faithfully, and trust You even when the path is hard. May my perseverance bring glory to Your Name.

Notes

My Discipleship Life Prayer

Father, make Jesus the central reality of my life:

1) Ignite in me a deep affection for Jesus, Your Word, and Your will in my life.
2) Fill my heart and mind with Your presence, power, wisdom, and love, in order that I might abide in You, so I can love You with all my heart, mind, body, and soul, and love my neighbor as I love myself.
3) Thank you for Your grace, sacrifice, forgiveness, and the gift of salvation that allows me to live confidently in the family of God.
4) Give me knowledge, understanding, and wisdom to make godly decisions, living in humble obedience to Your ways.
5) Give me strength, patience, and perseverance to reject the foolish values of this world, in order to love and worship You all the days of my life.
6) Produce spiritual fruit in me: love, joy, peace, patience, kindness, goodness, faithfulness, gentleness, and self-control so that I can live and walk by the Spirit, rejecting the sins of my flesh.
7) Allow my words and actions to help others believe the Gospel, drawing them to Christ.
8) Empower me to be bold, stand firm, walk faithfully, and endure all adversity to bring glory to Your Name.
9) **Help me to be grateful and satisfied with whatever I have.**
10) Lord, I surrender myself fully to You. Please create in me a clean heart, and renew a right and steadfast spirit within me.

Lord, heap blessing on me and my family today; bring peace, contentment, and rest into our lives and homes in order that our faithful service brings glory and honor to Your Name. Amen.

SECTION 10

Gratitude
and
Contentment

Prayer Focus:

"Help me to be grateful and satisfied with whatever I have."

Day 46
Learning to Be Thankful

Discipleship Life Prayer Focus
"Help me to be grateful."

1 Thessalonians 5:18 Give thanks in all circumstances; for this is God's will for you in Christ Jesus. NIV

Devotional Reflection

Gratitude is more than a response to favorable circumstances. It is a posture and attitude of trust. Scripture invites believers to give thanks in all circumstances, not because every situation is good, but because God remains present and faithful within them.

Today's reflection encourages attentiveness to God's daily provision. Gratitude shifts focus from what is lacking to what has been given. It softens the heart, calms anxiety, and strengthens faith.

This prayer asks God to cultivate a thankful spirit that recognizes His hand in both abundance and need. Gratitude is a discipline that trains the heart to notice grace.

Life Implications

A disciple oriented toward gratitude learns to recognize grace. Attention shifts from what is missing to what has been given, shaping perspective and reducing anxiety. Gratitude becomes a steady attitude rather than a situational response, producing contentment regardless of what life brings.

The result is a life increasingly anchored in trust; one that recognizes God's faithfulness as a daily reality rather than an occasional outcome.

Reflection Questions

1. What do I overlook when I consider gratitude?
2. Would practicing thankfulness affect my perspective?

Daily Prayer

Father, help me develop a grateful heart that recognizes Your presence and provision in every circumstance.

Notes

Day 47
Contentment as a Learned Discipline

Discipleship Life Prayer Focus

"Help me to be satisfied."

Philippians 4:11–13 I am not saying this because I am in need, for I have learned to be content whatever the circumstances. I know what it is to be in need, and I know what it is to have plenty. I have learned the secret of being content in any and every situation, whether well fed or hungry, whether living in plenty or in want. I can do all this through him who gives me strength. NIV

Devotional Reflection

Contentment does not come naturally, it is learned. Scripture reveals that contentment grows through experience, trust, and reliance on Christ. This scripture challenges the assumption that satisfaction comes from improved circumstances.

Contentment rests in sufficiency – not excess. It allows peace to exist regardless of external conditions. This prayer focus invites a shift from performance to trust. It suggests we should abandon comparison and focus on gratitude.

Learning to be content frees the heart from constant restlessness and opens time and space for joy.

Life Implications

Satisfaction does not depend on improved circumstances. Restlessness gives way to sufficiency as trust in Christ replaces the pursuit of constant improvement. Contentment challenges the impulse to strive endlessly for more.

The resulting lifestyle is one driven by quiet confidence, not dissatisfaction or anxiety. by quiet confidence. It is a life in which one learns to be content with God's provision rather than trying to accumulate more.

Reflection Questions

1. Where do I struggle most with dissatisfaction?

2. How does trusting Christ affect my sense of contentment?

Daily Prayer

Lord, teach me contentment that is rooted in Your strength and presence rather than in the results.

Notes

Day 48
Resisting the Trap of Comparison

Discipleship Life Prayer Focus
"Help me to be grateful and satisfied."

Hebrews 13:5 Keep your lives free from the love of money and be content with what you have, because God has said, Never will I leave you; never will I forsake you. NIV

Devotional Reflection

Comparison and jealousy will quickly undermine contentment. Scripture calls believers to be satisfied with what they have, grounding contentment in God's abiding presence rather than external or worldly treasures.

We must be aware of how comparison distorts perspective and fuels discontent. God's faithfulness is personal, not competitive. When we measure ourselves against others, gratitude fades and anxiety grows.

The request to be grateful and satisfied asks for freedom from comparison by anchoring trust in God's promises.

Life Implications

A life freed from comparison returns repeatedly to gratitude. Attentiveness to God's personal faithfulness reshapes how others' successes or circumstances are perceived. Comparison loses its power as daily habits of thankfulness and gratitude are established.

The result is a life increasingly marked by peace; one that integrates gratitude into everyday thought patterns and resists measuring worth against external standards.

Reflection Questions

1. Does comparison affect my sense of peace?
2. What helps me return to gratitude when I get caught up in comparison?

Daily Prayer

Father, free my heart from comparison and help me rest in Your faithful presence.

Notes

Day 49
Trusting God's Provision

Discipleship Life Prayer Focus
"Help me to be satisfied with whatever I have."

Matthew 6:31–33 So do not worry, saying, "What shall we eat?" or "What shall we drink?" or "What shall we wear?" For the pagans run after all these things, and your heavenly Father knows that you need them. But seek first his kingdom and his righteousness, and all these things will be given to you as well. NIV

Devotional Reflection

Jesus invites His followers to trust God's provision rather than live in a continual state of anxiety. We are reminded that worry often reflects misplaced focus. When we seek God's kingdom first, provision becomes a matter of trust rather than fear.

Trusting God does not eliminate responsibility, but it removes panic. This prayer invites confidence that God knows our needs and provides in His time and His way.

Provision becomes an expression of God's care rather than a source of control or manipulation.

Life Implications

The believer oriented toward trust and satisfaction learns to release anxiety about provision. Fear-driven performance is replaced by confidence in God's care and timing. Seeking God's kingdom becomes the organizing priority, determining how needs are understood and addressed.

The prayer seeks a life increasingly free from worry; one that rests in God's knowledge of our every need. We are confident He will respond with adequate resources for our daily needs.

Reflection Questions

1. What concerns challenge my trust in God's provision?

2. How can I practice trusting God more fully today?

Daily Prayer

Father, help me trust in Your provision and seek Your kingdom before all else.

Notes

Day 50
Resting in "Enough"

Discipleship Life Prayer Focus
"Help me to be grateful and satisfied."

Psalm 23:1 The LORD is my shepherd, I shall not want. KJV

Devotional Reflection

"The Lord is my shepherd, I shall not want" is a simple declaration that reflects deep trust in the ultimate source of our peace. It invites reflection on what it means to live from sufficiency rather than scarcity.

Resting in "enough" does not deny desire, but it affirms God's care and concern. When God is our Shepherd, provision and guidance will replace fear and striving. This prayer invites peace rooted in a relationship rather than one based on the accumulation of things.

Living from "enough" frees us to live generously.

Life Implications

This prayer challenges the belief that satisfaction requires accumulation. Scarcity-driven thinking will lose its hold as trust in God's shepherding care deepens. Resting in "enough" resists the impulse to measure life by excess or comparison.

Thus, life is marked by peace and generosity. We live from sufficiency rather than striving for more, confident in God's faithful provision in our lives.

Reflection Questions

1. What does "enough" look like in my current season?

2. How would truly trusting God as my Shepherd change my perspective and priorities?

Daily Prayer

Lord, help me rest in the truth that You are my Shepherd and that in You I have enough.

Notes

Section 10 — Reflection Summary

Gratitude and Contentment

This section has invited a slower, steadier way of living. It is one shaped by gratitude rather than restlessness. Gratitude has been presented as a posture that recognizes God's presence and provision in every season, rather than a reaction to circumstances. Contentment is something developed over time. It is formed by trusting fully in Christ.

A recurring emphasis throughout this section has been sufficiency. When gratitude is practiced, attention shifts from what is lacking to what has been given. When contentment grows, anxiety is rejected. This section has challenged the assumption that satisfaction comes from improvement, accumulation, or comparison, reminding us that peace is rooted in God's faithful care.

We have also addressed worry. Seeking God's kingdom first reorders priorities and places our needs within the larger framework of trust. Provision is an expression of God's attentiveness rather than a source of concern. Being comfortable with "enough" reshapes how life is lived and how generosity is practiced.

As you think about gratitude, consider not whether your circumstances have changed, but whether your perspective has. Gratitude and contentment grow where trust is exercised daily, allowing peace to take root even when life remains uncertain.

Reflection

- Where do I most struggle to practice gratitude?
- How does comparison affect my sense of contentment?
- What would it look like to rest more fully in God's provision?

My Closing Response

God, teach me to live with a thankful heart. Help me trust Your provision and release my need for more than You have given. Free me from comparison and worry and form in me a spirit of contentment that rests confidently in Your care.

Notes

My Discipleship Life Prayer

Father, make Jesus the central reality of my life:

1) Ignite in me a deep affection for Jesus, Your Word, and Your will in my life.
2) Fill my heart and mind with Your presence, power, wisdom, and love, in order that I might abide in You, so I can love You with all my heart, mind, body, and soul, and love my neighbor as I love myself.
3) Thank you for Your grace, sacrifice, forgiveness, and the gift of salvation that allows me to live confidently in the family of God.
4) Give me knowledge, understanding, and wisdom to make godly decisions, living in humble obedience to Your ways.
5) Give me strength, patience, and perseverance to reject the foolish values of this world, in order to love and worship You all the days of my life.
6) Produce spiritual fruit in me: love, joy, peace, patience, kindness, goodness, faithfulness, gentleness, and self-control so that I can live and walk by the Spirit, rejecting the sins of my flesh.
7) Allow my words and actions to help others believe the Gospel, drawing them to Christ.
8) Empower me to be bold, stand firm, walk faithfully, and endure all adversity to bring glory to Your Name.
9) Help me to be grateful and satisfied with whatever I have.
10) **Lord, I surrender myself fully to You. Please create in me a clean heart, and renew a right and steadfast spirit within me.**

Lord, heap blessing on me and my family today; bring peace, contentment, and rest into our lives and homes in order that our faithful service brings glory and honor to Your Name. Amen.

SECTION 11

Surrender and Inner Renewal

Prayer Focus:

"Lord, I surrender myself fully to You. Please create in me a clean heart, and renew a right and steadfast spirit within me."

Day 51
What Full Surrender Really Means

Discipleship Life Prayer Focus
"Lord, I surrender myself fully to You."

Romans 12:1 Therefore, I urge you, brothers and sisters, in view of God's mercy, to offer your bodies as a living sacrifice, holy and pleasing to God – this is your true and proper worship. NIV

Devotional Reflection

Surrender is often misunderstood as loss, but Scripture presents it as worship. To offer ourselves fully to God is not to diminish life, but to place it where God can shape it. Paul describes surrender as a living sacrifice, active, intentional, and ongoing.

This invites honest reflection. Partial surrender feels safer, but it limits transformation. Full surrender entrusts control and outcomes to God. It is not a single decision, but a daily posture of openness and trust.

Surrender is both freeing and challenging. Importantly, it is the doorway to a life aligned with God's purposes.

Life Implications

A life developed through surrender learns to release control without losing purpose. Trust replaces guardedness and allows God's direction to become more natural. Surrender shifts our perspective from self-management to attentive dependence on God. This allows life to be shaped and grown rather than defended.

The implication of this prayer is a life increasingly aligned with God's purposes. The believer entrusts outcomes and direction to God's faithful governance.

Reflection Questions

1. Which areas of my life are the most difficult to surrender to God?
2. How might surrender deepen my trust and freedom?

Daily Prayer

Lord, I surrender myself fully to You today, trusting You to direct my life according to Your purposes.

Notes

Day 52
Inviting God to Search the Heart

Discipleship Life Prayer Focus
"Search me and know my heart."

Psalm 139:23–24 Search me, God, and know my heart; test me and know my anxious thoughts. See if there is any offensive way in me, and lead me in the way everlasting. NIV

Devotional Reflection

True surrender welcomes God's searching presence. This reminds us that self-awareness has human limits, but God always sees clearly. Inviting Him to search the heart is an act of faith.

God's examination is never harsh or condemning. It reveals areas that need development or healing. The prayer invites honesty asking God to expose our hidden motives or our internal resistance.

When God searches the heart, He leads us into life, not shame, exclusion, or condemnation.

Life Implications

This prayer encourages you to be honest with God because He knows you better than yourself. Fear of exposure will give way to confidence in God's goodness and care. This attitude allows God to search the heart, which will challenge our avoidance and encourage honest engagement with what lies beneath the surface.

The implication is a life lived with transparency. It trusts God's searching work as a pathway to healing and renewal rather than judgment.

Reflection Questions

1. What might I be hesitant for God to reveal?

2. How will trusting God's love change my openness?

Daily Prayer

Father, search my heart and lead me in Your ways, trusting Your loving guidance.

Notes

Day 53
A Clean Heart Before God

Discipleship Life Prayer Focus
"Create in me a clean heart."

Psalm 51:10 Create in me a pure heart, O God, and renew a steadfast spirit within me. NIV

Devotional Reflection

A clean heart means renewal, not perfection. We should recognize that David's prayer is a request for inner restoration after failure. God's grace does not merely remove guilt, it transforms the heart condition.

The prayer recognizes that sin and weariness affect our inner life. A clean heart desires what honors God and resists what corrupts. Renewal begins with humility and repentance, opening the way for transformation.

God delights in restoring hearts that turn toward Him.

Life Implications

The disciple whose life is renewed by God's grace learns to attend to the inner life with humility. The practices of repentance and dependence become woven together into daily rhythms. Renewal is determined by how desires are controlled and how failure is addressed.

Thus, life is increasingly marked by responsiveness and regular returning to God for cleansing and restoration as part of ordinary discipleship.

Reflection Questions

1. Where do I sense a need for inner renewal?

2. What would a clean heart look like in my daily life?

Daily Prayer

Father, create in me a clean heart and renew my spirit to desire what honors You.

Notes

Day 54
Renewed Strength for a Weary Spirit

Discipleship Life Prayer Focus
"Renew a right and steadfast spirit within me."

Isaiah 40:31 . . . but those who hope in the LORD will renew their strength. They will soar on wings like eagles; they will run and not grow weary, they will walk and not be faint. NIV

Devotional Reflection

Weariness affects even committed faithful disciples. Fatigue may come from prolonged responsibility or extended waiting. Scripture promises renewed strength to those who wait and hope in the Lord.

A steadfast spirit is resilient because trust deepens and fear fades. The prayer invites God to restore endurance and stability where discouragement exists.

Renewal will often come through a faith perspective and reliance on His guiding hand.

Life Implications

A life oriented toward God's renewing strength demonstrates patience without resignation. Endurance will replace exhaustion as trust deepens in God's sustaining relationship. Weariness is met with renewed connection and reliance on God, not with withdrawal.

The result is a life increasingly steadied by hope and strength from God's faithfulness. It continues forward with patience and perseverance.

Reflection Questions

1. Where do I feel most spiritually or emotionally weary?
2. How might waiting on God renew my strength?

Daily Prayer

Lord, renew my strength and restore a steadfast spirit as I wait and trust in You.

Notes

Day 55
Living With a Steadfast Spirit

Discipleship Life Prayer Focus
"Renew a right and steadfast spirit within me."

1 Corinthians 15:58 Therefore, my dear brothers and sisters, stand firm. Let nothing move you. Always give yourselves fully to the work of the Lord, because you know that your labor in the Lord is not in vain. NIV

Devotional Reflection

Steadfastness anchors discipleship. Scripture encourages believers to remain firm and faithful, knowing that work done in and for the Lord is never wasted. Our lives and our ministry should emphasize consistency over intensity.

A steadfast spirit remains faithful through challenges as well as daunting uncertainty. This discipleship prayer invites long-term faithfulness, rooted not in personal resolve, but in God's sustaining power and grace.

God honors perseverance shaped by trust and faithfulness.

Life Implications

This prayer guards against inconsistency and discouragement. The temptation to abandon faithfulness when progress seems slow loses its influence. Steadfastness challenges the desire for immediate results, calling the heart toward perseverance that is based in faith and trust.

The result is a life shaped by enduring commitment and faithful service even in changing circumstances. The faithful disciple is confident God will honor steady obedience and is sustained by His grace.

Reflection Questions

1. What helps me remain steadfast in my faith?

2. Where do I need God's strength to remain faithful?

Daily Prayer

Father, strengthen my spirit so I remain steadfast and faithful in Your service.

Notes

Section 11 — Reflection Summary
Surrender and Inner Renewal

This section has invited a deeper look beneath our behavior to the inner life that shapes it. Surrender has been presented as acts of trust, placing control and outcomes into God's hands. Rather than a single act, surrender has been described as an ongoing posture, renewed daily as our hearts are opened to His restorative work.

A central emphasis throughout these days has been honesty before God. Inviting Him to search the heart acknowledges both our limits and His power. God's examination is for renewal, not condemnation. Where weariness or resistance have taken root, we have been reminded that God's grace meets us with patience and restorative power.

This section has also emphasized that renewal is part of God's work. A clean heart and a steadfast spirit are not produced by personal attention, but received through humility, repentance, and dependence. God supplies strength where endurance has worn thin and steadies faith when discouragement threatens commitment.

We have also affirmed the value of perseverance. A steadfast spirit remains faithful, trusting that work done in the Lord is never wasted. Inner renewal sustains obedience, anchoring faith during changing circumstances.

Consider not how fully you have surrendered, but how willing you are to remain open to God's renewing work—again and again.

Reflection

- Where do I find it hardest to surrender control to God?
- What signs of resistance do I notice in my inner life?
- How might God be inviting renewal rather than self-effort?

My Closing Response

Father, I place my life before You again. Search my heart and renew my spirit. Where I am weary give me strength. Where I resist teach me trust. Form in me a steadfast spirit that remains faithful and open to Your work.

Notes

My Discipleship Life Prayer

Father, make Jesus the central reality of my life:

1) Ignite in me a deep affection for Jesus, Your Word, and Your will in my life.
2) Fill my heart and mind with Your presence, power, wisdom, and love, in order that I might abide in You, so I can love You with all my heart, mind, body, and soul, and love my neighbor as I love myself.
3) Thank you for Your grace, sacrifice, forgiveness, and the gift of salvation that allows me to live confidently in the family of God.
4) Give me knowledge, understanding, and wisdom to make godly decisions, living in humble obedience to Your ways.
5) Give me strength, patience, and perseverance to reject the foolish values of this world, in order to love and worship You all the days of my life.
6) Produce spiritual fruit in me: love, joy, peace, patience, kindness, goodness, faithfulness, gentleness, and self-control so that I can live and walk by the Spirit, rejecting the sins of my flesh.
7) Allow my words and actions to help others believe the Gospel, drawing them to Christ.
8) Empower me to be bold, stand firm, walk faithfully, and endure all adversity to bring glory to Your Name.
9) Help me to be grateful and satisfied with whatever I have.
10) Lord, I surrender myself fully to You. Please create in me a clean heart, and renew a right and steadfast spirit within me.

Lord, heap blessing on me and my family today; bring peace, contentment, and rest into our lives and homes in order that our faithful service brings glory and honor to Your Name. Amen.

SECTION 12

Blessing, Peace, and Faithful Service

Prayer Focus:

"Lord, heap blessing on me and my family today; bring peace, contentment, and rest into our lives and homes in order that our faithful service brings glory and honor to Your Name."

Day 56
God's Blessing With Purpose

Discipleship Life Prayer Focus
"Lord, heap blessing on me and my family."

Numbers 6:24–26 The LORD bless you and keep you; the LORD make his face shine on you and be gracious to you; the LORD turn his face towards you and give you peace. NIV

Devotional Reflection

God's blessing is never random or excessive. It is intentional and purposeful. Scripture presents blessing as God's favor which is given to His people so that life may flourish under His care. God's blessing may include protection, peace, or His attentive presence.

We need a mature understanding of blessing. It is not merely material provision or ease, but the assurance that God is actively at work in our life for our good. This prayer asks God to bless us with the ability to live our best life in service to Him.

Receiving God's blessing begins with the understanding that we trust what He gives is best for our lives.

Life Implications

The disciple who lives a life blessed by God's provision learns to see blessing as stewardship rather than entitlement. Over time, gratitude replaces expectation and blessing is received as a means of growth and readiness for service. God's favor is understood as provision for faithfulness.

The benefit is a life increasingly oriented toward using God's blessing wisely, living with awareness that what is received is meant to support faithful obedience.

Reflection Questions

1. How do I accept and understand God's blessing?
2. How will God's blessing equip me to live more faithfully?

Daily Prayer

Lord, thank You for Your blessing on my life and family. Help me receive it with trust and live faithfully in response.

Notes

Day 57
Cultivating Peace in the Home

Discipleship Life Prayer Focus
"Bring peace into our lives and homes."

Colossians 3:15 Let the peace of Christ rule in your hearts, since as members of one body you were called to peace. And be thankful. NIV

Devotional Reflection

Peace does not happen accidentally. It is cultivated through intentional choices. Scripture calls believers to let the peace of Christ rule in their hearts. Such peace will naturally shape relationships and environments.

This prayer is focused on both our self and our homes. Peace grows where patience, forgiveness, humility, kindness, gentleness, and self-control are practiced. The prayer asks God to establish peace in order to provide Christ-centered harmony. It is a request to avoid conflict.

A peaceful home becomes a place of restoration and refuge.

Life Implications

This prayer addresses the tendency to allow tension, impatience, or unresolved conflict to define relationships. Choosing peace requires humility and intentional response rather than reaction. Peace does not prevent difficulty, but it governs how stress is handled.

The implication is a life increasingly shaped by Christ's peace. It is a life that resists escalation and seeks harmony through patience and forgiveness.

Reflection Questions

1. What disrupts peace in my home or relationships?

2. How can I allow His peace to guide my responses?

Daily Prayer

Father, let the peace of Christ rule in my heart and shape the atmosphere of my home.

Notes

Day 58
Rest as a Gift From God

Discipleship Life Prayer Focus

"Bring rest into our lives."

Matthew 11:28–30 Come to me, all you who are weary and burdened, and I will give you rest. Take my yoke upon you and learn from me, for I am gentle and humble in heart, and you will find rest for your souls. For my yoke is easy and my burden is light. NIV

Devotional Reflection

Rest is not a reward for finishing every task. It's a gift from God for the weary. Jesus invites His followers to come to Him, promising rest for the soul. This challenges the belief that constant striving honors God. He specifically says, "I will give you rest."

Rest restores perspective. It reminds us that our value is not measured by productivity, but by meaningful relationship. This prayer invites us to release burdens and trust in Christ's loving leadership.

Receiving rest requires a willingness to stop and be cared for.

Life Implications

We are called to integrate rest into our discipleship rather than treat it as interruption. Rhythms of rest reshape priorities while restoring attentiveness to God. Rest acknowledges our limitations and accepts His care rather than striving endlessly.

The hope here is a life increasingly balanced by peace and contentment, where rest supports faithful service rather than typical worldly values.

Reflection Questions

1. What keeps me from truly resting?
2. How might rest strengthen my faith and service?

Daily Prayer

Lord Jesus, I come to You for rest. Teach me to release my burdens and trust in Your care.

Notes

Day 59
Faithful Service in Everyday Life

Discipleship Life Prayer Focus
"That our faithful service brings glory to Your Name."

Colossians 3:23–24 Whatever you do, work at it with all your heart, as working for the Lord, not for human masters, since you know that you will receive an inheritance from the Lord as a reward. It is the Lord Christ you are serving. NIV

Devotional Reflection

Faithful service is rarely dramatic. Scripture reminds us that whatever we do – work, care, kindness, or responsibility we do it for the Lord. This affirms that ordinary faithfulness honors God deeply.

This portion of the prayer reframes service as worship. When service flows from gratitude and rest, it becomes sustainable and joyful. God highly values our faithfulness.

Everyday obedience becomes an offering of worship when it's done for Him.

Life Implications

A life oriented toward faithful service learns to value consistency over recognition. Ordinary responsibilities are approached with greater purpose as service is understood as worship. Faithfulness is expressed through attentiveness, integrity, and perseverance rather than recognition by others.

The result is a life increasingly shaped by devotion in daily tasks, one that honors God through obedience, faithfulness, and service.

Reflection Questions

1. Where has God called me to serve faithfully today?
2. How does viewing service as worship change my attitude?

Daily Prayer

Father, help me serve faithfully in every task, offering my work to You as worship.

Notes

Day 60
Living for God's Glory

Discipleship Life Prayer Focus

"That our lives bring glory and honor to Your Name."

1 Corinthians 10:31 So whether you eat or drink or whatever you do, do it all for the glory of God. NIV

Devotional Reflection

The discipleship prayer journey concludes with a clear purpose: God's glory. Scripture calls believers to live in a way that honors God in every aspect of life—ordinary and extraordinary alike.

Living for God's glory does not mean perfection; it means faithful intention. It means choosing faithfulness, gratitude, and trust daily. We are invited to live in the awareness that every moment belongs to God.

This prayer does not end a journey. It establishes a rhythm and way of life.

Life Implications

Today we must resist the temptation to put our faith in separate compartments. The desire to separate spiritual intention from ordinary life should give way to an integrated vision of discipleship. Living for God's glory challenges self-centered ambition and directs motivation toward what matters most.

The result of this prayer is a life shaped by meaning and purpose. It is one that consistently chooses to honor God in decisions, actions, and attitudes, recognizing that every moment belongs to Him.

Reflection Questions

1. What does living for God's glory look like in my life?
2. How can I carry what I've learned into the days ahead?

Daily Prayer

Father, may my life bring glory and honor to Your Name in all that I do.

Notes

Section 12 — Reflection Summary

Blessing, Peace, and Faithful Service

This final section has drawn the journey toward the life that is lived in response to God's provision. Blessing has been framed not as indulgence, but as God's purposeful care. Peace has been presented as Christ's rule within the heart and home. Faithful service has been shown as the natural expression of a life lived with gratitude and rest.

Our emphasis has been on receiving before acting. God's blessing steadies life so that service is not driven by anxiety. Peace provides the environment in which relationships can flourish and faith can endure. We are reminded that our value is measured by belonging to God, not service.

This section has also affirmed the sacredness of ordinary faithfulness. Service offered in daily responsibilities is often unseen and uncelebrated but it honors God deeply. Living for God's glory is not reserved for exceptional moments, but is expressed through intentional faithfulness in all things.

Today, your focus should not be on completion, but on continuation. This Discipleship Life Prayer is not meant to be finished, but lived. Blessing and peace remain ongoing gifts, renewed each day as life is entrusted to God.

As you arrive at the end of the 60 days, pause and consider what focus you want to carry forward into the weeks ahead.

Reflection

- Has my understanding of God matured?
- Where do I most desire Christ's peace to rule in my life?

My Closing Response

Lord, thank You for Your blessing and faithful care. Establish Your peace within my heart and my home. Teach me to rest in You and to serve faithfully in all You place before me. May my life—both the ordinary and unseen—bring glory and honor to Your Name.

Closing Reflection—Recommitment

Continuing the Discipleship Journey

Sixty days of prayerful reflection have now come to a close, but discipleship does not end here. What you have learned and practiced over these weeks was not a program to complete, but a posture to cultivate. The Discipleship Life Prayer is not intended to be confined to a devotional schedule, but to become a way of living your life.

Take a moment to look back. Consider where your heart has been impacted. Where has clarity grown or where does resistance still remain? Growth is often subtle. Some changes may feel small or unfinished, but even quiet shifts of desire and attention matter. God works patiently, forming faith over time, not all at once.

This journey has invited you to center your life on Christ. He wants you to abide in His presence, living in His grace, while walking faithfully through both ordinary and difficult days alike. It has asked you to surrender control by rejecting competing values, to bear spiritual fruit, and to trust God with both effort and outcome. None of this is accomplished through willpower alone. It unfolds through continued dependence on God's presence and grace.

Your commitment is not a promise of perfection. It is a renewed willingness to keep showing up, to listen, to trust, and to obey where God leads. You may want to return to this prayer regularly, to revisit particular sections, or to use it as a daily rhythm for ongoing worship and reflection.

A Recommitment Prayer:

Father, continue shaping my life around Jesus. Renew my heart where it has grown tired. Strengthen my faith where it has been tested and guide my steps as I seek to live faithfully. I offer myself to You, trusting Your grace, depending on Your presence, and committing to walk with You each day. Amen.

The Wisdom Prayer Series

Personal Daily Prayer Guide

Prayer Resource and Journal

This is a great resource to kick-start your prayer life!

Know what to pray.
Pray based on Bible verses.
Strengthen your prayer life.
Access reference resources.
Pray with eternal implications.
Write your own prayers if desired.
Organize and focus your prayer time.
Learn what the Bible says about prayer.
Find encouragement and advice on how to pray.
Reduce frustration and distraction in your prayer time.

Get your copy today!

https://www.amazon.com/dp/1952359260/

Can Prayer Change Your Life

Biblical Prayers That Transform the Christian Life

- Know God more deeply
- Trust God completely
- Seek God's wisdom for life's decisions
- Renew your mind through God's truth
- Grow in Christ-like character
- Live a holy life
- Love others as Christ loves
- Find strength in trials
- Live with eternal perspective
- Finish the race of faith faithfully

These prayers move beyond temporary needs and focus on the spiritual foundations that shape a life devoted to God.

Let These Prayers Shape Your Walk With God

Begin praying the prayers that will shape your life with God today!

https://www.amazon.com/dp/1952359813

The Wisdom Prayer Series

Prayers of Eternal Significance

You do not need to pray more words!

You need to pray with purpose, and eternal focus.

- Learn how to pray with eternal priorities.
- Refocus your prayer life around God's will.
- Discover prayers that shape decisions and daily direction.
- Pray with focus and meaning.
- Pray for spiritual growth, wisdom, and transformation.
- Strengthen your relationship with God.
- Pray for others with greater depth and eternal perspective.
- Discover transformational life-shaping prayer.
- Develop lasting and substantial prayer patterns.
- Prayers aligned with what matters most to you.

https://www.amazon.com/dp/195235983X

About the Author

After 25 years as an actuary, and 20 years as an entrepreneur, Steve began his third career as an author in 2020, when he published The OBSCURE Bible Study Series and in 2024 began publishing the Jesus Follower Bible Study Series. He is a member of The Church at Station Hill in Spring Hill, TN, a regional campus of Brentwood Baptist Church, Brentwood. TN.

This devotional book came about because one day for the fun of it he asked an AI tool to develop a 12-Day devotional from his personal Life Prayer for his own use. There was no thought of a commercial devotional book. Steve formulated a personal 25 word Life Prayer about ten years ago and now it is over 200 words and he wanted some additional material for his daily quiet time.

He found the result so useful that he developed this 60-Day Discipleship Devotional. We hope you find this meaningful in your devotional and prayer time.

www.getwisdompublishing.com

Contact Information and Links

The Wisdom Prayer Series

https://www.amazon.com/dp/B0GX31YV7f

Personal Daily Prayer Guide

https://www.amazon.com/What-Should-Pray-Personal-Journal/dp/1952359260/

Can Prayer Change Your Life?

https://www.amazon.com/dp/1952359813

The *OBSCURE* Bible Study Series

https://www.amazon.com/dp/B08T7TL1B1

The Jesus Follower Bible Study Series

https://www.amazon.com/dp/B0DHP39P5J

Get Wisdom – General Information

www.getwisdompublishing.com

NOTE: You Can Help!

Please leave an honest review on the Amazon Sales Page
https://www.amazon.com/dp/1952359791

Thanks so much

GETWISDOM
PUBLISHING

www.ingramcontent.com/pod-product-compliance
Lightning Source LLC
LaVergne TN
LVHW050957080826
845145LV00009B/2329

* 9 7 8 1 9 5 2 3 5 9 7 9 8 *